ALL THAT MATTERS

A Mother's Memories

Janis Hogan

CUMBERLAND HOUSE
NASHVILLE, TENNESSEE

Published by Cumberland House Publishing, Inc., 431 Harding Industrial Drive, Nashville, TN 37211-3160.

Cover design: Karen Phillips
Interior design: Don Farrell and Janis Hogan

Library of Congress Cataloging-in-Publication Data
Hogan, Janis, 1952–
    All that matters : a mother's memories / Janis Hogan.
       p. cm.
    ISBN 978-1-63026-030-9 (alk. paper)
     1. Parent and adult child. 2. Mother and child. 3. Adult children--Family relationships. 4. Mothers and sons. 5. Parenthood. I. Title.

   HQ755.86 .H64 2000
   306.874'3--dc21

                                   99-057375

Printed in the United States of America
1 2 3 4 5 6 7—05 04 03 02 01 00

This book is dedicated to:

My grandmother, whose innate goodness gave me something to aspire to.

My mother, who showed me every day of my life what love looks like.

My father, who convinced me that believing in myself was as easy as putting one foot in front of the other.

My sister, Joyce, who loves me and values me as a friend, even though I tormented her for the first seventeen years of my life.

My brother, Richard, who showed me by example that judging people is not my job.

My son Jason, who proved that a mother who made all her worst mistakes on her firstborn child can still produce a pretty terrific young man.

My son Bryan, who trusted me with his deepest thoughts and gave me the strength to let him go.

Lastly, to my husband, Don, who loves me fiercely and demands nothing in return, who made me believe in love again, and who proved once and for all that there is such a thing as a happy ending.

Well . . .

I was walking in the night
and I saw nothing scary.
For I have never been afraid
Of anything. Not very.

—Dr. Seuss, "What Was I Scared Of?"
Sneeches and Other Stories

Contents

Prologue

When I look at them now, I think they can't possibly be mine. They are so perfectly formed. It wasn't long ago that I was looking at forms like these with sensual longings. It wasn't long ago that men who looked like these wielded tremendous power over me. Perfectly molded male bodies. Profiles silhouetted against the night like paintings on Greek pottery outlined in black. They are perfect, and I am in awe. They are my sons. Men. Cheekbones carved with arcs so finely etched their smiles spring like jack-in-the-boxes—out of context, but jubilant. One has blue eyes, one has brown, and behind each set is a different hoard of mysteries. Behind each set is a wealth of treasures I helped them gather. One has the gift of analysis and persuasion, the other the authority of logic and sensitivity born of introspection. They both possess a characteristic more valuable than any others I may have wished for them— integrity. Some say I am very lucky—a single mother blessed with such good boys. I say it's not luck. It's work. It is painful. It is joyful. It is love, pure and simple.

Introduction: Memory's Sweet Surrender

About nineteen years ago I left the South and moved to the Northeast with a husband hell-bent on catapulting to the top of the corporate ladder. We dragged with us two little boys who pronounced "Dad" in two syllables and believed every house came with its own creek full of crawdads and minnows. As soon as they could fill out a college application they hightailed it right back there. Not long before that, their father folded up his corporate ladder and planted it in someone else's yard.

I'm still here, and as a consequence I can't stop by on Sunday afternoons to have tea with my mom like I did twenty years ago. I can't call my sister and say, "Hey, let's go downtown and try all the new perfumes till we find one we can't live without." I can't meet my Dad in the park for a Saturday morning jog, nor can I have my brother change my oil filter and show me the proper way to wash my windshield.

I have friends who think maybe I'm the lucky one. Because all this distance means I can't—like other families who never moved apart sometimes complain—get on my older son's nerves when I ask him to stop by more often or make my youngest son feel guilty because he spends more time at his girl-friend's house than his own. And my sister and I won't fight over who helped mom plant her deck garden last or who really ought to run over tomorrow and help Dad get the TV to the repair shop. We won't fight about it because she'll just have to keep on doing it all herself. And my mother can't stop by on her way to the grocery store and drive me crazy by telling me my linen closet is a disaster and how do I ever find the twin sheets. And my father can't sit on my couch and call me from the far corners of my house to ask me one more time why I refuse to get cable television. Maybe, they tell me, it's all just as well. But when my phone rings on a rainy Sunday afternoon and I hear my son's voice say, "I'm here at Nan and Pop's, you want to tell your father 'Happy Birthday?'" I don't feel like one of the lucky ones. I feel, instead, like the child that got left at the park and no one noticed until they got home and counted heads.

So nearly every day there is a quiet empty hum that drones in the back of my mind. It's the sound of their living, their day-to-day rituals, their casual exchanges, occasional irritations, voluminous laughter, hundreds and hundreds of minutes that I am missing. To quiet the hum I fill the space with flashes of time. I recapture everyone in my life in split-second vignettes from the past and freeze-frame them. Then I hold them to me like a bouquet of spring flowers. Each one precious, each one a unique fragile jewel.

In this sense my children and the rest of my family travel with me wherever I go. And although I have only two children and two siblings, my mind sees them in pictures and there are hundreds, even thousands. There is the toothless six-year-old with wet blue eyes who cried for days after seeing *The Rescuers*. There's the lanky twelve-year-old who finally hit a home run after six years of trying. Nearby, a cocky fifteen-year-old regresses to stammering in monosyllabic mumbles when the "awesome" blonde calls. And somewhere, hiding in the shadows, is his snickering brother who set the whole thing up. They share space with the crinkled little mass the nurse swore was my baby that howled at birth and didn't stop until he said his first word. Darting around the corner is my five-year-old Batman who ducked behind the Japanese maple to whip on his black satin bat cape.

They are all here, all of them my children, numbering now in the tens of thousands. Barely a moment of age separates them from each other, yet they are as distinct and wholly themselves as if they were an entire tribe of individuals. With them is my mother tossing a flirtatious laugh across the living room to my father who is singing "Fly Me to the Moon," into his golf trophy. She is wearing gold lamé stretch pants and a leopard print shirt and besides Lana Turner, I don't think anyone else could have pulled it off. My mother is also there with her first grandchild and my father is trying to teach me how to swing a golf club when I am eight months pregnant. My sister is there, fishing in a mountain lake and trying to ignore my brother who's shooting GI Joe dolls with his BB gun. And there's my brother in a tuxedo at his wedding, and in his first sport coat at twelve years old for mine. Only milliseconds away, my sister sits beside my bed telling me not to worry, that lots of people have miscarriages and still have tons of kids. And there she is, holding the one that weighed nearly a ton and was too big for the Christening gown she bought him.

I carry all of them with me because living nine hundred miles away from them often haunts me. It hurts most acutely when it's someone's birthday and everyone is sitting around my mother's dining room table but me. I think about it almost every minute of every day when I take a breath that feels only half full, because missing them is a hollow feeling that doesn't leave much room to breathe deeply. Sometimes, when it's cold and rainy and the fog won't seem to lift, this vague emptiness swells to an immense longing to hear them, see them, touch a cheek, clutch an arm, and I wonder if I will breathe at all. At times like these my husband of barely three years tries to be all of them, and I am grateful, but not assuaged.

For reasons that even they don't understand yet, my children gravitated back to the South near where they were born, where they hung Christmas stockings on their grandmother's mantle and played Yahtzee with my mother on her lime-green iron and glass kitchen table. One of them can be at my parents' house in little over an hour. The other can make it in three. And they do that quite often. I'm glad about that, and I sometimes wonder what it is that draws them. What is it that keeps this family so tightly bound? And then I have only to surrender myself to my memories to know. It comforts me between visits and phone calls. It gives me hope that some day the geographic distance that divides us will somehow diminish.

For more than twenty years I have chronicled my life and theirs with my stories. It helps keep the memories alive and close, reminding me of the value in every moment. There are thousands of moments I wish could relive. Just as many I wish I could unlive. The moments I tried to preserve in my stories are those that taught me something. Gleaming treasures of time that I may have passed right over when they occurred, but that glowed and sparkled with meaning when I rediscovered them. Many of my stories chronicle rites of passage. Some are triumphs; some are downright hurdles. Many of them still make me cry.

When my oldest son announced his intention to marry and settle in Tennessee, sealing that distance and making it real, I scoured my files for all the stories I could find about him and wept over all of them. It seemed then that I needed more than ever to gather all of my family around me and hold them near, as near as I could, at least on paper. The result is this book, my gift to myself, and in turn to everyone who has become a part of me, a shared breath. In this place, in each moment, we are together again. Always.

Author's Note: About the Chairs

For me and for this purpose, chairs are symbols of people moving through life. They represent a moment when hopes are born, dreams turn into goals, ideas become plans, promises are made. They are a place to mourn when promises are broken, a place to think, to wish, to daydream. We sit in these chairs and share our thoughts . . . or not. We wonder; we question; we express fears; we apologize; we berate ourselves or others; we congratulate ourselves or others. In them, for an instant, time stands still while we try to figure it all out.

All the chairs in this book are real and from a place that holds significant meaning for me—especially the two on the cover which were taken from a painting my husband did for me of a balcony where we sat watching the sunset and drinking red wine on our honeymoon three years ago. In "Dancing in the Dark" the rocker is identical to the one I thought would lull my newborn to sleep. (This one was photographed at the Cracker Barrel Restaurant in Massachusetts because mine long ago got moved to Vermont and stayed there.) The Chippendale in "The Harry Chronicles" sat beside my father's best friend's desk all the years I knew him. Now it sits beside mine. The lifeguard chair in "One Wrong Turn" still stands sentinel at Quassy Boat Club in Middlebury, CT. And the bleachers still play host to hundreds of mothers who huddle there as I did with their teeth clenched waiting for the next play at the junior high basketball game. The "miracle chair," thusly named because my father said it would be a miracle if he could sleep and he always does on this chair, continues to sedate anyone who lights upon it. The chair was, in fact, the catalyst for "The Father I Remember." Many of the stories began as memories inspired by a chair, therefore, many of the chairs have a direct relationship to the story. Others have only a symbolic association, related by a time or function. The University of the South chair in "Daddy's Home" belonged to my son's father when he was about the same age my son is in the story. Nearly all of the chairs are still very much a part of my life—in my parents' dining room, on their deck, in my kitchen, my bedroom, my family room, and anywhere else there's a corner for contemplating.

Through the magic of Photoshop and my husband's patience and skill, my chair photographs were painstakingly transformed into charcoal sketches and matched to the appropriate stories. My hope is that they add a bit of texture and dimension to the words that follow.

Part One

Dancing in the Dark

In the corner of Jason's room sits a rocking chair with a handmade afghan draped over the back. We bought the chair the day I found out I was pregnant and excitedly moved it into the living room. For months while we awaited his delivery, I would rock and dream of the day when I could hold him against me in this chair, when I would feel his back rise and fall underneath my hand. But from the first day we arrived home as mother and son, Jason decided he would find his sleep alone. After feeding him for the first time in his new home, I settled into the cushions on my new rocking chair and began the rhythmic back and forth motion I had rehearsed for six months. But instead of the relaxing, quiet drifting I had expected, I felt his body grow rigid. I felt his tiny hands, balled into fists, squirm between his chest and mine. Beneath my hand, the muscles in his back and neck tensed and I could feel his head turning to lift off my shoulder. Instead of quieting, he cried louder. His feet pedaled and his knees jerked as if he somehow needed to escape.

After weeks of experimenting with formulas, different rocking motions, different chairs, walking, standing, different rooms, we finally settled into our routine. I would put him down and leave the room. Only then would he sleep. During the day we enjoyed our mutual space and companionship. He grew and learned, smiled and laughed and talked. Occasionally, he would sit quietly in my lap and let me read to him as his fingers traced over colorful pictures on a page. But when the story ended, or he lost interest, he would arch his back and hurl his body downward until I finally put him on the floor or in his walker.

There must have been an underlying sense of longing in me, a need to be needed. Deep down, there was an emptiness in me I had successfully buried until my friend Irene came through the door with John.

Until that moment, I never knew that babies hugged back. I didn't know they would willingly seek you out and struggle to climb into your lap. I didn't know they could hold your face in their little hands and look into your eyes. Mine does none of these things. Instead, he summons me for the necessities in life. He cries when he's hungry and stops only when he's fed. He whines when he's bored and smiles again when he's entertained. And in between I can carry him from room to room, from the crib to the high chair and from the house to the car seat, but he doesn't tolerate more handling than that. Occasionally, when he bumps his head or closes his finger in his jack-in-the-box, he will cry and lift his arms to me for consoling. But I can only hold him until the sting subsides, and all the while he keeps his knees and elbows planted firmly between us.

I had looked forward to Irene's visit for weeks. Despite the six hundred miles that had separated us since our junior year in high school, we had stayed in touch through weekly letters and monthly phone calls. And since we had been best friends since the fourth grade, it seemed only natural that we would share the experience of our firstborn by giving birth thirty days apart.

When I opened the door to Irene, she handed her son to me with a look and sigh of total exhaustion. Immediately, he wrapped his pudgy arms around my neck and laid his head on my shoulder. "He's tired," she said, as if that explained this unexpected affection. "He didn't sleep all the way from Virginia."

For a moment, I was speechless. This precious creature had willingly surrendered to me and in that instant I was both captivated and relieved. This

18

was how I envisioned motherhood—a melding of two emotional and physical selves. Something in me released then, because I knew that whatever was missing was not being missed by Jason. There was not some deep forbidding chasm over which he was afraid to reach. He was simply taking all he needed from me. John would be John, whether he was with his mother or me. I placed my hand on John's back and patted him gently. He did not budge. In my mind I thanked him for the experience and for the freedom it would give me from that day forward.

Throughout their three-day visit, Irene and I remarked often on how different the two boys were. While John was quiet and content to sit on the floor with a small collection of toys, Jason was in constant motion. John still had not spoken a word. Jason was repeating sentences. When they left on Sunday afternoon, John reached out to me and planted a soft kiss on my mouth. Jason said, "Bye, John," and waved.

Today the memory of John's sweet affection has faded, and Jason and I have returned happily to our respective spaces. He smiles and laughs when I speak to him and has learned to recite the poem that hangs above his changing table. He is a happy child in perpetual interaction with everything and everyone. Everywhere we go, he watches intently—his surroundings, the people, and me. If I leave a room he follows me. If he can't, he calls for me. He is certain I am never too far from him, but the space that separates us is his. "Sit here, Mommy," he says patting the couch near his pile of Legos. "In a minute," I answer. "I have to get the laundry." He drops his block and watches me as I turn the corner to the laundry room. Seconds later, he's standing at the door. "Towel," he says, pointing to dryer. "That's the dryer," I say, closing the door. "This is a towel." I wrap the warm blue towel around him and lift him into the air. He laughs and lets me carry him back to his blocks.

One day he is fretful and unusually quiet. I glance at the rocker in the corner of the room and for a fleeting instant it lures me, but I dismiss it as a lesson learned. By mid-afternoon his fever is palpable. Don't worry, the doctor assures me, this bug is going around. Jason pushes his food away at dinner and by 6:30 is crying incessantly. At 7:00, I am crying with him. I put him down

19

early and stand outside his door and listen intently behind it, waiting for him to settle. For nearly five minutes, I hear him thrashing. Several times he stands and shakes the crib. Tiredly, he calls out a few words, none of them "Mommy." Finally, he's quiet and I sneak back in to check his blankets.

Standing beside his crib, I strain my eyes against the dark. Only a thin sliver of light from the hallway slides under the door. He's lying on his stomach with his head turned toward the wall and I can't see his face. But I know his fist is pressed up against his mouth. His hair is slightly damp and lies featherlike over the collar of his terry cloth sleeper. His back rises and falls in rhythmic sequence. I want to reach out and rub his back—to somehow let him know I am here. But I don't. Afraid of waking him, I back up quietly and slip out the door.

Later, his cry splits the night like lightning. I find him in a tangle of wet blankets crying with his head pressed against his mattress and knees tucked under his stomach. I change him, coax a few drops of medicine into his mouth and carry him to the living room. "Moon," he says hoarsely, pointing toward the window.

In the dark, I reach blindly for the switch on the stereo and Dave Loggins's whispery voice wafts through the shadowy room. "Please come to Boston . . ." the Tennessee singer pleads.

"Dance," Jason says, swinging his head around and leaning toward the music.

"Okay, Buddy," I say, shifting him to my left hip and taking hold of his left hand. "We'll dance for a while." His tiny hand is hot and sticky. Already, I can feel the heat radiating from his body. I start to dance, bouncing him with the rhythm of the guitar. He giggles weakly. With the little strength he has left, he holds his body tensely against mine as if he were a dance instructor leading me around the ballroom floor. The album plays through while we move in concentric circles around the couch. "Moon," Jason says again, reaching toward the window. I stop long enough to restart Dave Loggins before waltzing Jason to the window and turning so he can watch the moon.

When my husband stumbles from the bedroom to find me, it's 5 A.M.

and Jason and I are standing beside the picture window. The moon casts a long shadow in front of me that sways across the living room floor in fluid motion as I rock my weight back and forth. Jason sleeps deeply, his nose tucked against the place in my neck where the pulse throbs close to the surface. His left hand is limp at his side and his right one is balled up against his mouth. There is no sound. The music has long since stopped.

"Why didn't you wake me?" my husband asks peering at us through half-opened eyes. "Do you want me to take him?"

"No, that's okay," I answer, whispering. "He's asleep."

"Why don't you put him down, then, and go back to bed for a while? I'll get him if he wakes up again."

"In a minute," I say, tightening my arms around the sleeping body. "This is the first time I've been able to rock him to sleep." My husband smiles knowingly and kisses us both on our foreheads. "Call me if you need me."

I reach over and turn the music on again. "Just one more dance, Buddy," I say to my unmoving partner. And we dance until fingers of pink light pull away the darkness and morning fills the room.

21

The Legacy

When I come in from school, my mother is standing at the sink peeling carrots. Her back is rigid. She is only five feet two so she doesn't have to bend at all. The peelings tumble in graceful orange arcs into the sink like miniature divers back-flipping. My mother runs the sheathing silver tool toward her, just as her mother did. I have never mastered it. It feels backwards to me. My ineptness causes more of the carrot to be wasted, she assures me. I don't like carrots anyway.

She turns when she hears me drop my books on the table. "Hi, sweetie. How was your day?" She doesn't expect answers and she doesn't stop the rhythmic motions. In my peripheral vision, I see her move to the stove where pans are simmering at the right temperatures above stainless steel rings and drip pans that gleam as if they had never been used—as if gravy or chocolate pudding had never bubbled over the edge of the pan. I don't have to see her to know she is wearing something like green linen pants with an ivory georgette blouse. The kitchen floor tells me she is wearing her black patent leather pumps with pointed heels that make her look taller. I know too, her hair has just been brushed and sprayed and that if I went into her room I would smell the remnants of Chanel mist that failed to cling to her as she breezed from the room.

I might walk over to her and kiss her on the cheek, but it doesn't occur to me. This is not my time. This time belongs to my father. My mother's nightly ritual as she prepares to welcome him home is as natural and necessary to her as the tide coming back at noon.

Sometime between five and six o'clock, he floats in looking as pressed and polished in his charcoal suit as he had when he left the house that morning, his after shave less pungent but still aromatic enough to let us know he is in the room if we don't seen see him first. My father is the presence that changes not just the smell, but the very weight of the air we breathe. When he's home, it's as if the house has been plugged in. Every movement and every word now has a purpose. My mother's smile is more relaxed, her movements are lighter. It's as if my father's reentry seals us in and she feels safe again.

Without even a sideways glance, he moves deliberately to my mother and captures her with arms long enough to encircle her twice. Next to him, she appears diminutive but not frail, and it occurs to me that he is a good foot taller than she is. It's something I forget when they are distanced by the span of a room. She laughs, and plays at brushing imaginary lint or water droplets from the lapel of his suit. She knows I'm here; he pretends not to. She's coy and embarrassed and backs away after receiving his full kiss. They are both well over forty and I think the whole thing is perverse. Both because it's a word I just learned and because I know nobody else's parents act that way.

Only after she backs away does my father turn his attention to me. "You're so quiet I didn't see you there," he says.

Even now, that vision is as clear to me as if it had been filmed and played over and over at family gatherings. It is, in my mind, a defining moment in their relationship. In that scene, my father is acting out a promise, a belief, maybe even a code that he's chosen to live by. Quite simply, my mother was number one in the order of things. And it took me somewhat by surprise, because I knew it was not the way she saw herself.

In retrospect, this scene that took place more than twenty years ago just now makes sense to me. Throughout my years as middle child in a household, I struggled to find my place in the family long before I dared exert my power in the world. I remember the day my sister set out to prove she was the favorite child. "Dad, if we were all on a boat and it started to sink, who would you save first, me or her?" My sister rarely spoke my name out loud. If she did, it was usually contorted in some fashion to rhyme with something foul. Mostly she called me, "her."

"I'd save your mother," he said, without taking the amount of time we expected he should have pondered. In fact, it seemed he didn't think mournfully at all at the prospect of losing us.

"Oh, Daddy," my sister lamented. "What if Mommy wasn't there?"

"Then I wouldn't be there either," he said. "I hate boats." We had to be content with that. Even as a five-year-old, I knew well enough to appreciate a small comfort when it was handed to me, and I was glad to know I would not be sinking to the bottom of the ocean alone. But while it was clear that he was avoiding an answer, he was also sending us a message—one that we would hear thousands of times, in thousands of ways.

The idea of my mother in first place was a concept I had never considered. In my mind, my mother's life was a series of fulfillments, but none of them hers.

"Mom," I would plead, "I have a test on capitals tomorrow. Can you help me?" After the dishes were clear and my father was parked, dessert in hand with the newspaper in his lap, she'd sit across the counter and drill me, backwards and forwards.

"Missouri," she'd say, looking me dead in the eyes as if she could send me the answer.

"Darn, I always forget this one. Give me a hint."

"Think 'misery,'" she said, cajoling. "Jeff is in misery."

"Jefferson City!"

The next day she'd be waiting at the door at 3:30. "Well, how'd we do?"

"We made a ninety-eight," I'd answer, fully believing it was as much her "A" as mine.

Even now, thinking back over a lifetime, I'm hard pressed to come up with a time when my mother's desires or comfort were given precedence over anyone else's.

Every morning throughout our school years my mother went out into the carport in her bathrobe to warm up the car while my sister and I ate a breakfast that had been laid out for us. My mother hated mornings and didn't talk much. Nonetheless, she would no more allow her children to shiver against the cold leather seats than she would have had us wait outside for the school bus that passed by our door an hour earlier.

"You know, your mother and I walked to school when we were your age," my father would chide as we scurried into the car. "Yeah, Dad, we know. Three miles in a foot of snow," we'd moan.

If we were home from school sick, she'd drag extra pillows from her bed, plump them up behind us and flatten out the blanket to accommodate any number of board games we felt like playing—the game boards exchanged occasionally for tea trays bearing toast and soup. In the span of a day, we'd easily experience the entire contents of the game closet. If she had scheduled a lunch or a shopping trip, she canceled it.

Typically, we were less appreciative of the devotion than we should have been. Worse than that, we may have interpreted our mother's attention as a sign that she had little else to do. We simply didn't understand the order of our universe. Often, my father felt it necessary to remind us of my mother's place in it. "Do not think of putting that fork in your mouth until your mother sits down," he'd say, glowering. "Who left a coat in the living room?" he'd bellow from the hallway. "Your mother was not put here to pick up after you."

The romantic drama played out in our kitchen twenty years ago changed the way I viewed my parents. But it was also the day I began to build expectations for my own future. I knew that when my father came home that night, he and my mother entered a world of their own, just as they had every night since they met and married. It seemed to me strange, but also magic. It was something I wanted for myself.

In the years since, especially during times when I showed up on their doorstep severely wounded from shattered hopes and crushed illusions, I came to know my parents had not really lived the unbroken dream sequence I carried in my mind. There had been times of desperate pain—times when my mother believed she had fallen to last place and when my father felt as if he didn't have a kind word or smile left to give. But the fact that we never saw it does not feel like a lie to me. Whatever the moment contained, whether it was charged with anguish or contentment, anger or compassion, my brother, sister, and I saw nothing but mutual respect and honor between them.

I remember lying on my bed with the phone tucked between my shoulder and ear listening to my best friend complain about her parents fighting. "Don't your parents ever yell?" she asked.

"Well, sometimes," I answered. "But not at each other."

"No, huh. What do they do?"

"They dance."

"They what? Did you say dance?"

"Yeah, they're doing it now."

I could barely hear the music sliding under my door. It could have been Tommy Dorsey or Glenn Miller. The records were a hundred years old and they all sounded the same to me.

"No way," she said. "You mean like slow dance?"

"Yeah."

"Wow," she said, in a tone that sounded uncharacteristically sympathetic. "That's too weird."

"I know," I answered. "Don't tell anybody, okay?"

"Don't worry. I won't. But hey, which do you think is worse, the yelling or the dancing?"

"I don't know," I said. "But if it were me, I think I'd rather be dancing."

Buried Treasure

It was hot that day—so hot even the wind refused to move. I sat perched on the bottom right corner of my bed, so I could just catch the breeze as the fan swung in a slow arc back and forth between my parents' room and mine. My sister sat in the middle of her bed encircled by comic books. She didn't seem to feel the heat, which was fine with me, because usually we would be fighting over whose side of the room got the most fan air. Each time she turned a page of comics, she held her right hand in front of her and tilted her head. There on her fourth finger was a gold ring bearing a tiny rectangular emerald. "You better take that off before you lose it," I said in my purposely irritating little sister voice. "Mom said you could wear it to church. Church is over."

"You're just jealous," she said snidely, "because she's never let you wear it." She was probably right. I was jealous. But then again, I never would have asked to wear it, because I never would have wanted the responsibility. That emerald was the only real treasure my mother had. She kept it in a pale green music box on top of her dresser. When we were younger, she would gather us onto her bed and lift the lid on the box so we could hear the tiny brass instrument inside play "Swan Lake." But my sister was always more interested in the ring. She would pick it up and look deeply into the dark green emerald. "Tell me about the ring again," she would say.

So my mother would tell us again about her father and how he struggled to keep his construction business going during the depression—often accepting barter in lieu of payment. And how her mother had spent hours each week mending used clothing to take to the church for children of families whose jobs had not survived the depression. Because of that, her parents were not inclined to want or give "frivolous" things. But still, when her birthday came around, they presented her with the one thing she longed for, a tiny, perfect emerald ring—her birthstone.

"Come on, we're going for a ride," my father yelled down the hall of our two bedroom apartment on that hot June Sunday. His voice was loud enough to carry over the clattering hum of the old fan. My sister looked up from her comic book and scrunched her face into that "oh, brother" look. "How are we going for a ride, Dad?" she yelled back. "We don't have a car."

I sat across the room and stared at her, waiting for the boom. If you had something to say to my father, you went to where he was and said it politely. My sister was eight at the time, two years older than I was, and I knew she knew that. She tossed me a smirk and returned to "Millie the Model." When footsteps thundered down the hall, growing louder as they passed the fan, she never even flinched. I thought she was very brave.

"Come on, girls. We're going sailing on a yellow bird." My father's voice, almost singing, filled the room before his foot crossed the threshold. My sister looked sidelong at me with a smirk that clearly said, "Got you!" I guess she knew that even though my father said he had eyes in the back of his head, he couldn't hear a small voice over a clattering fan.

Outside, parked alongside the curb was a pale yellow convertible with the top down. My mother stood holding my brother; neither of them moved. My sister and I stopped on the steps, both of us with gaping eyes and mouths. My father was the only thing in motion anywhere—waving his arms excitedly. "Come on, Harry loaned it to us for the whole day!" he said sounding much like I felt the day I got my first two-wheeler.

And what a day it was! Until then, my road travel had been restricted to ten blocks on a school bus. Most of our extended family lived within walking distance, and those that didn't, came to see us. That day in the yellow convertible, I felt as if a door to the world had been opened for me. I don't think I spoke a single word as lakes, forests and farm land spread out in front of us and swallowed the huge yellow convertible in swirls of vibrant greens, yellows, and blues. My mother sat in the front, wearing a huge scarf tossed casually over her head with the ends twisted and wrapped loosely about her neck. I thought she looked just like Grace Kelly in *To Catch a Thief.*

Unhampered by seat belts, my sister and I knelt in the back seat and watched the world roll away from the back of the car. We waved to everyone like Miss America on parade and dreamed of the days when we would live in one of these big white houses with porch swings hanging from sky blue ceilings and red geraniums in the window boxes. I thought even my sister was impressed with the yellow convertible and the magic it brought, because she never once looked at the ring on her finger.

The sun had turned orange and purple by the time we got home. My brother was asleep on my mother's shoulder. My father lifted me out of the car without opening the door—ruffling my hair as he lowered me to the sidewalk. Turning back to lift my sister out, he stopped. She sat huddled against the seat with her head tucked between her shoulders. Although I couldn't see her face, I could tell by the way her back quivered that she was crying. He picked her up and held her against his shoulder.

"I lost it," she kept sobbing, over and over. "Lost what?" my father asked helplessly. I knew before she said it. My eyes darted to her right hand that was then clenched tightly around my father's neck. The ring was gone. My brother was awake now, squirming in my mother's arms, but she seemed not to notice. She was staring at my sister. Leaning over slowly, she stood my brother beside me. "Take him inside," she said. I took his hand but didn't move. I knew my sister was going to catch the devil, and I didn't want to leave her alone with them. "Go!" she said, shooing us with her hands. I took his hand and edged up the walkway, craning my head over my left shoulder. I saw my mother take my sister from my father's arms. It was a strange sight. At five feet two, my mother was not much bigger than the sobbing eight year-old, yet she seemed at that moment as strong and tall as my father who towered above all of us. My sister clung tightly to my mother shaking her head back and forth. My mother held my sister's chin in her hand and kissed her on the fore-head. I never heard what they said and I never heard anybody yell. For a moment I felt a twinge of disappointment.

Seconds later my sister ran past me into the house. My parents stayed outside for a while. I guess they were looking through the car for the ring, because the car had to go back to Harry that night. Nobody ever talked about it again, but I know they never found it, because the next time I crawled up on my mother's bed to open the pale green music box, "Swan Lake" played, but there was no emerald inside. Over the years, I would find new treasures in the box, three baby teeth, a tiny ceramic violet my sister made in art class, a four-leaf-clover my father found in the back yard.

These days when we get together for holidays or someone's birthday, we sometimes talk about the day my father borrowed Harry's convertible, and how my father had pretended to be John D. Rockefeller surveying his estates. We laugh and try to remember the words to "Someone's in the Kitchen with Dinah," because my mother says we sang it at least fifty times that day. She never mentions the emerald ring. For a long time I thought it was because it made her sad to remember it, but now I realize that's not it. My mother knew even then that there would always be new treasures to put in the music box, but there would never be another day of sailing in the yellow bird.

 # The Son Also Rises

At 7 A.M. Monday, I am gently awakened by the slight pressure of miniature cold hands on my face. "Come on, Ma," my youngest son Bryan demands. "You have to get up and go to school."

Dragging my resisting eyelids open, I see his older brother Jason, who is holding my morning tea and scowling at my reticence, has joined him.

"Remember, Mom, you told me to make sure you got up in time to finish your homework. I told you, you should have done it yesterday." He is delighted with his new self-appointed role as guardian. While I, on the other hand, am wondering if I can transfer upstate and complete my remaining eighteen credits in a dormitory, away from the scrutinizing eyes of my six- and nine-year-old sons.

It's at times like these that I berate myself for doing things backwards. I could have spent all of my college years under the tutelage of my parents who were, as I recall, much less demanding than my children are.

Not once did my mother call from home to ask if I was attending class regularly, doing my assignments or studying for exams. The one year of bona fide university life I spent in a dorm conjures up only memories of blissful unrestrained freedom and bi-weekly letters from my mother asking if I had enough money.

My children, however, are not content to let me struggle through unsupervised. "When is your test, Mom? Are you sure you studied enough? When is your paper due?"

Neither are they satisfied with mediocre performance. Like dwarfed master drill sergeants, they push me, badger me, and shame me into excellence. "Mom, I really think you should do that drawing over. It doesn't look like a pear." Or, "Not a 'B'! Come on, Mom, you can do better than that!"

After weeks of their unyielding expectations, I find myself haunted by the desire to impress them. At the same time, I'm finding their standards more and more difficult to attain. I'm flat out tired of homework, and I feel like slacking off for a while. At 3:30, when I hear the loud squeaky brakes of the public school bus, I drop the phone, leaving my girlfriend in mid-sentence at the other end, grab my European History book from the kitchen counter, and dive for the couch. Slacking off is one thing. Getting caught at it is another.

"How was your test, Mom?" Jason bellows from the door. "Was it really hard? I don't think you studied enough." And while he lectures me on the importance of good study habits, it occurs to me that I haven't seen one of his spelling or math tests all year. Just as I am about to counter attack, he says with a smirk, "By the way, isn't it about time I had a conference with your teacher?"

He's kidding, isn't he?

34

Career Counselors

Monday morning I hear the familiar sound of little feet descending hardwood stairs. It is 6 A.M., and I know that only because my husband just left in his running clothes after waking me to tell me, "It's only six o'clock, go back to sleep."

It's a Monday in August, summer, the season of slumber. A time when children don't have to be wrested from the clutches of twisted sheets and blankets. A time when mothers can have their coffee in the kitchen instead of under a dripping umbrella at the school bus stop. A time for late breakfasts with Phil Donahue or Gary Collins and afternoon swims that last until salad and sandwich dinners. Why, then, is my nine-year-old son now standing at my bedside with a cup of steaming tea and an ear-to-ear grin?

"Mom, you told me to wake you up if you were still asleep. Aren't you going to work today?" Jason, my oldest, does not try to disguise the impatience in his voice as I strain to emerge from my semi-comatose state and remember what day it is.

I remember then. I am going to work. It's my second week and still the routine of getting myself dressed and groomed is foreign to me. The tables have turned. Instead of me diving through debris under my son's bed searching for his missing sneaker while the bus rumbles impatiently outside, he is glaring at me and drumming his foot as if I am the recalcitrant child.

"Okay, okay, I'm coming." It's been more than ten years since I worked outside the home. In fact, you could say, it's my first real job—my first experience in my chosen profession. I might have managed to put it off a few more years if my children had not pointed out the newspaper office two blocks from our home and challenged me to begin the journey up my career ladder.

Jason and his six-year-old brother Bryan had spent the last two years comparing their life with a stay-at-home mother to that of their friends. Even though I have often been the only mother home in the various neighborhoods in which we've lived, it never became an embarrassment to my children until we moved to New York. It seems that here, in the land of professionals and matching Audis, I stood out like a sore thumb.

"Mom, I had to write a story about my parents and what they do and I couldn't do it," Bryan cried one day after school. "You don't do anything."

Jason, my shadow, who won't go into the grocery store alone because he's afraid I'll forget he's in there and leave him, said, "You know, Mom, you could get me my own key so you could get a job and I could take care of Bryan." This is the same Jason who lost three jackets and a watch at school in less than three months and who says to his brother daily, "If you don't shut up I'm going to break both your arms."

On the way to the library one day, Jason pointed out the *Daily News* building as we walked by. "Mom, you could work there, you know. You're almost finished with school. You said you wanted to be a writer."

"I suppose I could," I said. The idea held more glamorous than practical appeal. I pictured myself in Lois Lane efficiency and style, commanding the attention of a bustling newsroom. "Sure," I said, "I'm sure they are waiting for someone like me. I'll go in tomorrow."

Naturally, I didn't. The idea seemed more preposterous and frightening the next day. And just as naturally, my children refused to let me off so easily. "Did you go yet, Mom? I told my friends you were going to work at the paper."

"Oh, Jason, you didn't," I said annoyed that my lack of courage was not going unpunished. "There's no way they're going to give me a job."

I was, of course, more annoyed with myself that the very words I use to motivate my children would haunt me unmercifully unless I faced my fear and went. "You are only a failure when you refuse to try."

So, the next day, I gathered my sparse portfolio, unearthed my only pair of intact panty hose and drove two blocks (I could have walked but I wanted to look really professional) to the news office. It just so happened there was an opening, and it just so happened it was part time, and wasn't it a coincidence that I happened to walk in just as they were composing the copy for the "help wanted" ad?

Now my children are smug and satisfied as they rally around my bed to push me into the world of the gainfully employed. They struggle to get a look at my paycheck on Thursday with visions of Disney World and twelve-speed bikes dancing in their heads. I suggest they make a copy of their wish list for the baby sitter, since she receives half of my salary.

Exactly two and a half minutes from my home by car, I sit at my desk at the newspaper filling out my official time card. I call home to tell Jason I would like to work until 1:30 this afternoon, putting in a full 15-hour week. Could he, I ask cringing with the horror of my intended neglect, possibly manage for half an hour without the baby-sitter?

In the pause, I can visualize his gray eyes blinking, fighting a flush of tears. "But Mom, you said you'd be home at 12:30. I want you to come home." Another few seconds of silence pass before he adds, "I miss you."

"I'll be right home," I say. I guess Lois Lane will have to wait.

37

Everlasting Love

"Promise me," I pleaded. "Promise me we'll always be like this. That twenty years from now we'll still want to make out on the couch." I stared into my future husband's eyes and clutched his arms. It was one month after my nineteenth birthday and one day before my wedding. "If you can't promise me that, I can't go through with it."

He laughed and he promised. He said he couldn't imagine a time when he wouldn't want to be near me every minute of every day. A time when he wouldn't want his hands to travel every inch of my body.

Eight years later, I found myself longing for his touch. Asking him why he was so cold, so distant. Why did he sit up all night in front of the television and leave for work without waking me? Finally gathering the courage to ask the forbidden question. "Don't you love me anymore?"

"I love you," he said, painfully, sadly. "But I'm not in love with you."

If he had slammed a baseball bat into my stomach, I would have felt the impact less than I felt those words. I was doubled over, struggling for air. It was days before I slept or ate. Weeks before an intelligent thought surfaced in my consciousness. I simply throbbed internally like a new bruise.

Later, much later, when panic began to ease and rational thinking returned, I realized that I had reached the same conclusion at least three years earlier. I too had sat up nights alone wrestling with the same emotions. Is this all there is? Where is the passion, the longing? Where are the butterflies I used to feel when his body came near me? Where is the fire that used to erupt inside me when his lips pressed against mine? Somehow, I had worked through it without ever saying a word. For a while I dreamed of faceless passionate lovers. For a fleeting moment, I toyed with the notion of seducing the carpenter who smiled at me and tossed his sun-streaked bangs whenever I asked how the new deck was progressing. Or even simpler, responding more enthusiastically to his suggestive banter. I could have. He would have. It would have been exciting. It would have been a disaster.

There were months of desperate loneliness, endless hours of silent tears. It was a time of mourning. And then, a time of healing. It was, in a sense, a weighing process. In the end, I had compiled a list of unspoken but indisputable facts. He was a strong, independent, sometimes kind and considerate man. He was also silent, over-ambitious, and often blindly obsessive. He was the father of my children. Although there were no longer sexual flutters when we kissed, or surges of heat when our eyes met, there was a comfort at the sight of him, a reassurance in his touch. Added to that, there was the delight in my son's eyes when the screen door opened and a voice thundered down the hall, "Daddy's home!"

In the days that passed after my husband's declaration of dying love, I embarked on a relentless crusade to stack the deck in my favor. If he's going through the same weighing process, I reasoned, I have to tip the scales a little.

I ironed shirts before he asked for them, sewed buttons that were only loose. I learned how to hang wallpaper, refinish furniture and bake bread. I finished college, took up jogging and became a blonde. I toiled hours in the kitchen making soup no one else but he would eat. I clipped coupons and spent the money I saved on a cashmere coat for him and a sexy nightgown for myself. For a few months it seemed to make a difference. We had fun again, wrote love notes on birthday cards and made love in front of the fireplace. And then, the novelty wore off. For every plus I accumulated, he could find another minus.

Why weren't the children bathed before I had to leave for class at night? Why did I have to complain every time he wanted to play golf both Saturday and Sunday?

Now suddenly, we are facing another anniversary, and the cold silence encases us again in our separate enclaves. We orbit individually around the children like Pluto and Jupiter vying for the sun's warmth. Strangely, I know I love him no less than I did the night I pleaded for unending passion—more, in fact. But still the space between us fills with dark blue coldness, and we repel with violent force when we pass.

There are few published words relating to marriage and relationships that I have not digested and committed to memory. I have read and conversed with more marriage and relationship counselors than you're likely to see in a full yellow page. I believe I have confronted the truth face to face, and have long since forsaken any illusions I may have had regarding the institution of marriage. In short, I have stopped chasing windmills. I have also stopped earning pluses from my husband.

I've learned a lot from the experts, but more, I think, from a simple, honest appraisal of where we are. I know we resent the qualities that once attracted us to each other. I know that love requires work, communication, and compromise. I know that passion cools to comfortable familiarity and desire wanes and peaks. I know that couples unconsciously try to resolve conflicts they grew up with by reliving them in their marriages. But knowing all this doesn't seem to help. You have to believe that it's all okay anyway. You have to believe that basically, you're both pretty neat people and that the family you've created is worth working through the disappointment that love is not a continual high. The thing I know with the most surety is that my husband doesn't believe any of this.

So, forget trying to tell him he's haunted by a past he can't reconcile, and by a vision of romantic love he can't let go of. Maybe if he had grown up with a mother and a father and seen a relationship at work he would not believe, as he does, that disagreement equals mutiny. If he had ever seen how compromise fuels a loving relationship, he would not be so sure everyone else is wrong all of the time.

Last week I called a friend to thank her for a thoughtful birthday present. She was depressed and distracted. "I'm going to a marriage counselor Tuesday," she said.

This can't be, I thought. If her marriage ends, there is no hope for the rest of us. I've known her since we were twelve years old and watched her marriage develop and mature over ten years. I had never been in the company of a couple who supported and encouraged each other as they did, openly and without reservation.

"Ben says he loves me, but he's not in love with me anymore."

It was difficult to suppress a cynical chuckle. "Tell me," I coaxed, "have you been running around madly trying to earn points?"

"God, yes. How did you know?"

"And do you feel like a broken Diana Ross record singing 'I'm gonna make you love me' over and over again?"

She laughed. She knew exactly what if felt like. Why, she wondered, didn't anyone ever warn us that we were going to fall out of love? Why do we all grow up believing that all we have to do to achieve perfect bliss is to marry the right person? Why, we both want to know, do men have such a difficult time making the transition to everlasting love?

It seems our husbands share a common trait. They are both ambitious workaholics. They are driven and preoccupied with success. They are also, therefore, surveyors of situations, receiving and evaluating data relating only to surface emotions. If they are uncomfortable or unhappy, they look around for the cause. We are there, therefore, we are the cause.

My husband says he feels neglected. I am not the woman he fell in love with. I can't argue with that. I am now the mother of two. I am a college graduate with a brand new part-time job and I have found a dry cleaner that does his shirts better than I ever could. My hair is brown again, and I only make soup we all like. I still jog, but I don't hang wallpaper myself and I don't go to marriage counselors alone anymore.

Today, nine hundred miles away, my friend battles with similar phantoms. She is sitting in a chair talking to her first marriage counselor, her legs twisted in pretzel links beneath the chair, her purse strap wrapped like a noose around the first two fingers of her left hand.

"My husband isn't in love anymore," she'll say, the tears forming in the corners of her eyes. The counselor will smile in understanding. She may even

42

say, as mine did, "You're marriage isn't on the rocks dear, it's just lost its fizz."

She'll begin the journey then. She'll do a lot of talking, reliving, explaining, and then nodding. Saying, "Yes, I know." Because she does know. Already. She understands the phases of marriage, the instability of emotions.

Later tonight, her husband will walk in and stare at her, looking for a sign, a hint that a cure is taking place in her. He knows she went for help. She asked him to go with her. He declined, holding fast to his belief that the problem is hers. If she can get fixed, become the girl she was when they met, he will fall in love again. He wants that. Believes it is his right.

My friend and I have high hopes. We are sad a lot of the time, because we are needy. We are living with husbands who give nothing because the fire of love is not compelling them. They haven't learned, as we have, that love is an action verb, not a state of being. That love requires the expenditure of personal energy and sometimes tireless effort.

They don't know how to reach out when they feel like caving in, how to transform a feeling of oppression into a hug, isolation into a touch. They still don't know that the measure of love is not what you feel but what you give.

Still, we are waiting. I can't give up, I tell her, until he says he will not, cannot learn to love from the mind and not the heart.

In the meantime, I am teaching my children the truth about everlasting love. "Dad isn't very romantic anymore," my youngest said just the other day.

"Romance is nice," I say, smiling. "But it's not everything."

It is, according to Webster, "not practical; an exaggeration or falsehood." Honestly, I looked it up.

"We're working on something better right now." I added, reaching out to cradle his face in my hand.

He seemed comforted by that. And, sometimes—when I take the time to think about it—so am I.

Colliding in Place

Separation anxiety. I expected it when I put my first child on the school bus for kindergarten. And again when my youngest started pre-school. I knew I'd have to face it again, probably worse, when the children went away to college. But nothing, not even the *Oprah Winfrey* show, could have prepared me for the day my husband moved out.

He was always fond of surprises. At Christmas he'd hide my presents or save a special gift for later in the day. Once he surprised me at work with a picnic lunch. Last month he surprised me with a simple statement. "I've seen a lawyer, and I'm moving out."

A simple, uncomplicated, concise compound sentence. Eight words that carried with them the destructive force of a nuclear bomb. In one instant the mortar that bound my life together shattered, and all the pieces tumbled to a heap at my feet.

There's no point in describing the pain. You could hear it in words a thousand times described by the literary giants of our time in a thousand ways. And still, you'd have only the faintest notion of the unbridled searing that rips through your chest.

It goes on and on. Hour after hour. Day after day. I've heard it best described by my friend Kathy who compared it to being skewered alive and pinned to a board like an insect specimen. No matter where you turn or twist, no matter how you writhe and tug, you can't get away from it.

And because you know full well that each child you have to tell will be skewered on the board beside you, you plunge another stake in your own heart. You take the pain that spills from them; you reach for it, wishing with all your heart that you could take it all, and you shove it all into the gaping hole that was once your heart, where it throbs and festers.

And you think with the telling the worst is over. It isn't. It's the empty closet, the empty dresser, and the empty bed. It's the roaring dark emptiness in the night. It's reaching out to the person you'd always turned to and clutching only air. It's the memory of his face.

Every day when you wake up you tell yourself there can be nothing new to hurt you; the worst is behind you. But every day brings another first.

Tonight is the first night the children will spend with their father. When I come home from work, I see the sleeping bags and overnight cases piled by the door. I see the unmasked excitement in their eyes begin to cloud when they see the hurt in mine. I reach somewhere down inside me, pushing beneath the bilge of pain and anger to dredge up some compassion, some cheerful encouragement to free them from me—to let them know I will be fine. I tell them I want them to have a good time. I tell them it will be fun having Daddy all to themselves. I lie. Despite my good intentions, my attempt is feeble.

I hear the familiar sound of his car's engine approach and I am unreasonably startled when the doorbell rings. He no longer feels free to open a door on a house we built together. Tonight I am nearly blinded by the sudden slap of reality. We are now two separate families. When I open the door and see on the other side of it a man I've known well over half my life, it occurs to me that at this moment, my life has split in half. I will never again be free to run my fingers along his chin. I watch his hands as he reaches for the boys' things and know they will never again reach for me. I remember the feel of his chest against my back while we slept, the weight of his arm across my side, and I think I can't stand here looking at him another second without screaming.

But I do. I watch the door close behind the family I was once a part of, and I feel the whole sixteen years of its history crushing me like the foot of an elephant. I back into the hallway and slide down the wall to the floor. There I sit until there are no more tears left.

Today is the first day I am alone. The memories burn bright and hot from that hole in my chest. What did I do? What didn't I do? The thoughts of regret and guilt pour in like so much salt. I struggle to look forward. To put one foot in front of the other. Pick up the toys scattered on the floor. Put the dishes in the dishwasher. Don't think. Just move. But the images keep coming. Memories hurl like video flashes across the walls. Images of good times scramble to the surface, and over and over I push them back. I need to remember the times I suffered. The times he let me down. I need ammunition to kill the love that fans this pain.

For a while, I sit and watch the clock. I remember when weekends went by too fast. This one has already lasted a lifetime and it is only Saturday. I picture myself in the future with someone else. We are sitting in a restaurant nervously conversing over a glass of wine. The scene is ludicrous. I haven't been touched by another man since I was sixteen. Could the man who is divorcing me really be the sixteen-year-old boy that cried when I said I wouldn't take his senior class ring?

Unexpectedly, they are back. They forgot the skis. While the boys scramble for their gear, he stands for a while in the kitchen. He smiles pleasantly and his casual friendliness showers me like shards of glass that slice through the surface of my skin. The hurt that emanates from me horrifies him. Why am I making this so hard for everyone, he wants to know. Why can't we just be friends?

And I picture chatting with this friend over coffee, me listening to pieces of his life with my replacement. This man who made love to me in the shower—who wept with joy the first time he held his son—who promised to love me long after time had ravaged my body. This man is walking into my future with someone else. Can I smile and wave him along on his journey? I think not. Not now.

For now, I need to make a conscious effort to make the love die, and I can't understand why it's taking so long. After months of lying untouched

47

beside him, months of sitting up nights alone, months of being pushed away and criticized, night after night of waiting for him to come home for dinner, I am amazed at the tenacity of my love.

Still, my heart skips a beat when I hear his voice. When I'm near him my body screams in longing for the touch of his hand. In his presence I am complete. When he walks away, I am severed in two, and half of me is dragged behind him.

"He has a power over you," my thirteen-year-old says. "And he knows it. You have to stop letting him do this to you."

What kind of conversation is this to be having with your child, I ask myself. "You watch too many talk shows," I say, knowing he's right but trying to sound unconcerned and cheerful. But worse than that, knowing my pain is casting a cold dark shadow over every moment I share with my children.

Today, before my eyes open, I know it is still with me. It seems to defy the laws of human endurance. I think it cannot get worse and still allow me to keep on breathing, but it does.

This morning, at 3 A.M., I watch my youngest son toss and turn under his blanket and I wonder what shape this torment is taking in his dream. What a legacy we offer these children, I think, not raising a hand to wipe tears from my face. We show them only what to want, but not how to keep it. We show them they must only love someone until it is difficult, and then they are free to turn and walk away. We show them only to give while they are receiving and only to love those who are easy to love.

I walk back to my room and sit on the bed. The darkness offers me no comfort. There is no place to hide. I run my hand along the blankets where his body used to lie and I imagine his hand sliding out from under the covers to hold mine. Inside me pain thunders against my chest. Soon, I tell myself. Soon it will stop. I lean back against the pillow, close my eyes, and wait.

Table for Three

The room is warmly familiar. And even though we don't know anyone here, these people seem to be extensions of the warmth. They look up when we walk through the door. Many of them nod an acknowledgment. The smell of bacon drapes us immediately. It's a smell we will take with us on our clothes for most of the morning. Right now it's comforting. Later I know it will be less so.

"How many?" the waitress asks smiling with outstretched arms that balance four plates. I saw a trick like that when I was a kid watching the *Ed Sullivan* show. All this woman needs to match it is a stick between her teeth with a large white plate spinning atop it above her head.

"Four," I answer, without hesitating, my eyes riveted to the three sausage links rolling dangerously close to the edge of the plate closest to me.

"Mom?" Jason's voice interjects, lilting in a question—as if he means, "Are you okay?" Instead he states the obvious. "There are three of us."

"Oh, right," I laugh. "Three."

She gestures with a chin that ripples a few times as if to emphasize the direction she's pointing. "Take that one over there by the window, Honey. Looks as if you need a little sunshine this mornin'."

We sit—my two sons and I—after some awkward silent maneuvering. They are careful not to leave the empty chair beside me. For a split second, they can't decide where it should be. In the end, Bryan sits on my side of the table and Jason across from me. I am beside the window. The waitress is right.

I need this sun. It slices a diagonal slab of bright white across the table and spills over me like an old blanket. It is approaching seventy-five degrees outside, but I am often cold anyway.

The boys are scanning the menu. I am watching the sidewalk. Maybe this wasn't such a good idea, I'm thinking. When we decided, the three of us, to get away for the weekend, it was the immediate answer. It seemed a good place for regrouping and getting on with things. Although I've never lived here, this town has always felt like home to me. And although I don't know a single inhabitant by name, these people all feel familiar. I never knew why. But because this town kept calling me back after every ski trip or August week on the lake, my husband and I decided to buy property here. So today, my sons and I walked three blocks through town from our Victorian house on Pleasant Street to have breakfast. It will be the last time I do that with them. In a few weeks the house will belong to their father, and the one in Connecticut will be mine.

Today, I think, we are experiencing the end of a way of a life. This is our first step. Together for the first time, just the three of us, we have left the safety of our home and ventured out unmonitored. We've been here a dozen times, but still, we are pioneering. Together we bought the map, charted our route all on back roads, stopping anywhere we thought looked interesting. This moment, in this familiar place, I realize I'll be making all of my decisions for myself from now on. If there's supposed to be a sense of accomplishment here, I don't feel it.

Instead, I feel like a sentence without a verb. As if everywhere I turn, every move I make is incomplete. I try to push that feeling away, because I know that empty chair is haunting my sons more in its glaring stark silence than it would if it began rattling and shaking on its own. And I know too, my emptiness is the medium that conjures up this spectre.

Until today, my sons, at ten and thirteen, have known no other way of life. When we go to church it is two by two. When we go to dinner, there are four place settings. On vacation there are always four wave runners, four tickets to Disney World, four lift tickets. Today is our first public appearance as a threesome and we seem about as steady as a table missing a leg.

50

For a few moments, they avoid my eyes and concentrate on the menu. A waitress, a smaller one with only one very pointed chin and no trace of a smile appears beside me. "Will someone be joining you?" she asks. I am startled, both because she appeared with the suddenness of David Copperfield, and because the question is unnerving. It sends us hurling backward over the territory we just spent the past ten minutes arduously navigating. A simple, innocent question, and yet it confirms for me our blatant and apparently obvious incompleteness.

Bryan's mouth quivers slightly, but he makes no sound as he puts his menu face down on the table. Jason looks at me and then at the glowering waitress whose pencil, poised in a claw-like grip, hovers like a miniature spear above her pad. "No," I answer, smiling as much as I can force it. "It's just three."

As soon as I've said it, I know. A defining moment. A confining adverb. That we are described as "just" three is the problem—as if we are individually diminished by the absence of another.

A deep wave of sadness threatens me and the prospect of fighting it seems as difficult as backing out of a one-way tunnel. I look at Bryan and notice his eyes are fixed on the top of the mountain. From his seat, the chair lift is just visible above the tree line. I wonder if he is remembering our first ski trip. I turn my head to follow his gaze. In my mind I can see, as if it were yesterday, a smaller version of this child—bundled in neon orange and resembling a faded life raft—sailing down the beginner's slope. His skis are fixed in a tight bottomless triangle, and his arms flail like the wings on the wooden ducks they sell from roadside stands at the beach.

I realize I am laughing, and when I turn away from the mountain to face my children I am finally certain of at least one thing: that the memory I just relived is no less valuable than the ones we are creating now. And that the moment we are living is one I can cherish five years from now if I can just let myself live it. I don't know anything more than that except that I am hungry—really hungry for the first time in almost a year.

"Hey," I say, clapping my hands together in a gluttonous Henry VIII fashion. "I'm having the blueberry pancakes with extra bacon."

"Get out," Jason says, curling his lips in disbelief. "You'll never eat that."

"Right, Mom," Bryan says, back in the present moment. He picks up the forgotten menu and studies it. Then a smile crosses his face. "I'll bet you can't eat all three pancakes."

"Oh, really," I say. "What are you betting?"

"If you win," he says, "I'll pull all the weeds out of the sidewalk myself."

"That's pretty big stuff," I say, knowing that everyone in the house hates that particular chore worse than any other you could name. The bricks in our homemade sidewalk seem a more fertile ground for vegetation than the most prolific of all farmed fields in Connecticut.

"Yuck, Bryan," Jason chides. "You're nuts. I hope you lose so I don't have to do it."

"And what if I lose?" I ask Bryan, relishing the idea of my prized, heart-shaped walkway totally free of intrusive dandelions for as long as this lasts.

"You have to play 'Dungeons and Dragons' with me every night for a week."

I grimace and Bryan smiles ear to ear. In that smile I find a surge of strength and a wave of gladness pours over me like a welcome warm shower. This feeling lasts only a second—as bright and fleeting as the flash of a lightning bug. But for now it's enough, because I believe, really believe now, that like the lightning bug it will flash again.

"Come on, Bryan. What kind of a bet is that?" Jason taunts. "You know Mom loves that stupid game."

"Really?" Bryan says rather than asks, still smiling before turning back to his menu.

New Plans for an Old Holiday

Ask a woman to name her favorite holiday. That will take some time. She'll try to think of a holiday that's really a holiday—one for which she is not obligated to stuff, bake, wrap, or hang crepe paper, one that epitomizes Webster's definition to the fullest, "a day in which one is exempt from work." She will, in all probability, not say "Thanksgiving."

In my house this year there is only one adult orchestrating Thanksgiving. And while that fact could have caused my children and me some emotional distress, we decided to look on the bright side of things. For myself, I see some instant advantages, not the least of which is the power to outlaw television and excess labor.

The children are working up some enthusiasm by attempting to establish precedents. We are, they assure me, going to re-navigate old paths of habit and develop new traditions. This presents tremendous opportunity for experiment and change. And in my household, where furniture is rearranged so often the rugs have no time to dimple under table legs, change is as vital as breathing.

"Let's do something really radical," says Bryan while absently leafing through his car magazine. "Let's go to a concert."

Radical is evidently the word of the week for eleven-year-olds.

"Get real," intones the much older, much more mature brother. "That's anti-American. You have to stay home. We'll rent all the *Star Trek* movies ever made and eat turkey sandwiches and potato chips."

A picture of my grandmother's dining room flashes through my mind. I am sitting near the head of the immense mahogany table in a circle of aunts, uncles and cousins, all impatiently waiting for the last of the serving platters to be squeezed onto the lace-covered surface. I scan the walls of the room near the ceiling where my grandfather built a continuous plate rack for my grand-mother's plate collection. I count each one, stopping longer at my favorite: the white one with silver edging and wedding bells in the middle. I reach the last plate just as my grandmother takes her seat beside me.

I cringe to think of my children conjuring up memories of potato chips and alien space ships when they remember holidays past. "No audio visu-al aids for this holiday," I say.

Moans and then silence. Creative energy diminishes quickly when the use of electronic devices is removed from the list of options.

"Well, if we have to stay home . . . I mean, it is Thanksgiving," Bryan whines. "We might as well have a dinner."

"If we do, can we eat in the dining room and use Grandma's table-cloth?" Jason asks, forgetting his previous disappointment. "You know, the one that has the stain on it from the time Pop dropped his glasses in the gravy boat?"

Since they were old enough to sit propped in a high chair, my children have shared Thanksgiving with family. Their grandparents, aunts, and uncles, as well as my aunts and uncles and cousins in various configurations and num-bers, found their way into our home no matter where we lived—from Tennessee to South Carolina and then to New York. In the past few years, we've moved farther north, and relatives are traveling less. This year, there will be three for dinner. We're sticking close to home so the boys can celebrate the holiday at home with me and then later with their father. Even without the concert, it's a radical change for all of us.

"And Mom, I can make the mashed potatoes," Bryan says. This is the same child who can't open a cereal box without dumping half of the contents on the floor. "I learned how in Home Ec."

"Right," says Jason. "And who's going to scrape them from the ceiling?" There's a competitive edge in their bantering. "If he's making the potatoes, I'll make the stuffing."

"That's easy," Bryan says, adding a grunt for emphasis. "It comes in a bag. You just add water."

I shake my head, wondering if democracy is, after all, the appropriate approach here. Shifting my attention to my kitchen window, I notice the few leaves that are anchored stubbornly to the trees are stirring, resisting the pull and push of the November wind. I know the smell of winter is in the air. If I opened the door, it would come rushing in. With this season comes an inexhaustible supply of memories, dredging with them an equal number of emotions—the full range from childish delight to adult melancholia. And I know the combination of all of them is what makes us whole.

Just as I know that, I know we can't avoid the sadness associated with this change by trying to make this holiday "radically" different.

Back in my past for a moment, I see my grandmother taking her seat closest to the kitchen door. Her Thanksgiving prayer, which traditionally lasted no less than five minutes, draws to a close, signaling unspoken permission to dive into the serving platters. The chink of silver forks against fine china chimes throughout the room. These are the same dishes that arrived unscathed all the way from England in my grandmother's trunk when she was barely sixteen and crossing the Atlantic with her father on a crowded ship. The pale pink tea roses would always remind her of her mother's garden.

"You know, kids, this is beginning to sound like a regular, old Thanksgiving to me," I say, wondering what happened to their enthusiasm for chartering a new course for historical holidays.

"Yeah, it is," says Bryan, tossing the car magazine aside. "So we should use your grandmother's silver. Do you want me to get it out of the closet?"

"Hey, neat," says Jason. "And we can use the pink flowered dishes.

This year there will be enough." He crosses the dining room to the plate rack where the three surviving dishes stand side by side. Carefully he lifts them down one at a time and carries them to the sink.

"Mom, do you think we could use the wedding bell plate?" Bryan asks, reaching toward the plate rack with one foot off the ground. "It's my favorite." I watch and hold by breath as I hold my tongue. Hand painted beneath the silver wedding bells is the inscription, "Arthur and Marie, 1907."

My grandmother is, to my children, just a collection of stories. They never sat in her dining room counting plates or listened as she described the stone-bordered rose garden she would never see again. And yet, they know her.

My silence worries them, and they both turn to stare at me. I smile. I am thinking that we will not be alone after all. We will bring to the table multitudes—people they have never met as well as people they love. They smile back.

"This will be great, Mom," Jason says, turning back to rinse the pink flowered dishes.

"Radical," Bryan agrees.

And already, it is.

Wheels

Tonight my son asked if he could go to the mall with his friend John. Ordinarily, I wouldn't hesitate to give permission. But this time the request was qualified. John, Jason assures me, never drives over fifty-five on the interstate and always comes to a complete stop at stop signs.

This addendum both stuns and horrifies me. When I envision my children and their friends engaged in self-transportation, I see little red tricycles with squeeze horns on the handle bars, or at most, tall shiny twelve-speeds with micro-thin tires.

When, I wonder, did John stop sailing down my driveway on two wheels?

Outside I see quite a different vehicle. The hugely ominous machine armored in gleaming silver lies in waiting for my child. Headlights shoot white light through the black night like a fairy tale dragon breathing fire. It rumbles and growls—a giant angry dog crouched and ready to spring.

I look at this child of mine standing in the doorway, and I notice his head is only inches away from touching the top of the doorframe. Yet it seems only yesterday that he strained and stretched to reach the pedals on his first two-wheeler.

"Well Mom, what do you think? John's waiting."

Now I picture John poised behind the wheel of this killer machine. The impish grin I remember is replaced by a sinister leer. This boy on whom I lavished multitudes of praise for his kindness and charm has suddenly been transformed into a junior Mr. Hyde, metamorphosed, no doubt, by the vapor of gas fumes and burning rubber.

My son, quite attuned to my protective nature, does not push the issue with impatience. He has earned the wisdom of his fifteen years by losing battle after battle. Logic, regardless of its power in the universe, does not necessarily supplant mother's reasoning.

He is half-smiling, half-wincing in anxious anticipation, and this pose immediately invokes the memory of the day he learned to walk.

He stood shakily, his hands clutching the coffee table, and locked his eyes on mine. There I sat, just three feet from him, but to this child—so dependent, and yet so desperate to be mobile—the distance seemed an endless chasm. He smiled then, the same smile, filled with the joy of a new adventure, constrained somewhat by fear of the unknown.

"I'll call you when I get there if you want," he says. "And we won't be gone more than two hours." I look at him and once again his eyes lock onto mine. But this time I see the step from the other side. In his eyes I see a silent prodding, a patient encouragement. His eyebrows arch and his head nods, and I know, in his way, he is reaching his hand out to me and saying, come on Mom, it's not so scary once you let go.

I smile back at him, a smile not of excitement or adventure, but of resolve. "Sure, you can go. And you don't have to call me. Just be home by 9:30."

His face brightens, and he leaps forward to kiss me good-bye. "I'll bring you a surprise," he calls back over his shoulder as he thunders down the hall.

Alone, I try to erase the image of the fearsome metallic monster blazing through the night with my son, a willing captive, at its mercy.

The Date

It's some time before I realize he's not coming. It is, in fact, nine o'clock, and he's just about two hours late before I allow myself to accept it: I have been stood up. Call it naiveté, call it stupid, call it the first date I had, or almost had, in sixteen years.

"You know my friend Arnold?" Marie asked me one day during coffee. "You know, the one I told you climbs rocks?"

"Sure, I remember Arnold. He's the guy that stands as if he's about to do a pirouette. His knees turn sideways."

"Really? I never noticed that," she said frowning as if she'd just found a hair in her salad. "Anyway, Arnold said he was out with his friend last week for dinner and ran into you. He says his friend Mark wants to ask you out."

Rolling my mind backwards to visualize the previous week, I saw images of all the faces I'd encountered slip by like a film on rewind. Then it stopped suddenly on Arnold and an obscenely handsome man standing beside him. I knew we must have been introduced, but in the scene my mind replayed, there were no words spoken. There was only a gaze into the clearest, most intense blue eyes I have ever seen.

"You've got to be kidding! Mark can't be more than twenty-eight."

"He's twenty-six, and he's definitely interested. Do you want Arnold to give him your number or not?"

The question was not as simple as it sounded. A gorgeous male sees you in a restaurant; thinks you're hot, and wants a date. This is the stuff fairy tales are made of, unless you happen to be, like I am, thirty-six and married all of your adult life. When I was Mark's age, I had already been married seven years and had two children.

"Marie," I started, still not believing that a twenty-six-year-old soap-star look-alike and part-time rock climber had even noticed I was in the room, "I think your friend Arnold is confused."

"Never mind," Marie answered. "I'll just fix everything myself. We'll meet for a drink and I'll prove to you he knows exactly what he's doing."

And so she did, and he did, and he actually asked me out. I don't know what we talked about over this drink. I don't know how three hours slipped by so quickly without my being able to recollect an intelligent word sequence uttered, by me or anyone else. But, now, three days later, I am preparing for my first date since my eighteenth birthday.

Twenty years had skirted by me. Twenty years of changes to a societal ritual I was never comfortable with in the first place. I realize I don't know things like: should I have given him my address? Should I have met him somewhere instead? Do I offer to split the check? Do I invite him in? The last time I had a first date, we believed a French kiss marked us as "easy." The sexual revolution exploded around me while I was too busy changing diapers and navigating pre-schools to notice. Today, even in PG movies, the heroine has sex on the first date.

Deep down, I know this whole exercise is just my way of drying the ink on my divorce papers. Two weeks ago I signed them. Two weeks from today, my husband of sixteen years will be drinking champagne at his second wedding. My two sons will have a stepmother and a second place to call home. This date isn't revenge, I tell myself. It's just sheer delight that someone actually found me attractive enough and interesting enough to ask me out. I mean, someone who could get a date as easily as I could pluck laundry detergent from a grocery store shelf.

Saturday at 11 A.M., I calculate that I have about eight hours to get ready. The house is quiet; deadly in fact, and I have to find some way to occupy my time. Conjuring up "what if" scenarios is making my palms sweat, and the more I think about it, the less I like the whole idea of a stranger coming to this front door, ringing the doorbell and. . . . Well, there's the problem. What happens next? I can't remember how I did this twenty years ago and I'm not sure I want to know how it's done now.

For most of the day, I distract myself by finding things to clean. Whenever my emotional balance is off kilter I try to gain control of my environment. I guess I think if I can bring order to my physical surroundings, I'm somehow restoring order in my soul. It never works, but I keep the house pretty clean that way. For the first hour, I vanquish cobwebs left undisturbed since my last emotional frenzy. I wash the kitchen floor with a sponge and apply butcher's wax with a paper towel. While I wait for that to dry, I dust every light bulb and doorjamb top in the house. Buffing the floor with a dishtowel is especially effective. It doesn't shine as well as it would if I used the electric buffer, but it burns a lot more energy. By 5 P.M. I am hard-pressed to find anything that doesn't sparkle.

I take a long bath. Or at least it seems long, and by 6:15 I have tried two colors of eye shadow, four dresses—opting for cotton with a hint of Lycra for firmness—and five pairs of shoes, because Mark was sitting most of the time and I can't remember how tall he is.

At 7:05, I close my lips on the third shade of lipstick and sit in the living room to wait. I want to see the headlights when they come down the driveway. I want time to take deep relaxing breaths so I'm not shaking when I answer the door.

At 7:10 I open a bottle of wine. At 7:12 I open a bag of pretzels.

At 7:15 the phone rings. I lunge for it, sending the bag of pretzels scattering like a vicious game of pickup sticks across the polished wood floor. It's my mother.

"I know this is your first weekend home alone since the . . . you know. Since the papers."

"The papers," spoken in a hiss, sounds more distasteful than the term it is meant to supplant and brings to mind an image of my mother house training our boxer.

"Divorce, Mom, you can say it. Really. I can take it now."

I pace while we chat, and I think I effectively mask my agitation. At last, she is sufficiently reassured I am not gong to ingest drain cleaner or fall into a catatonic depression. I decide against telling her I have a date with a young man I could have given birth to. Okay, maybe not. But I could be his aunt. When she hangs up I know she is shaking her head and wondering what she can do to cheer me up. Her sigh is cut off just as the phone hits the cradle.

At 7:30, my rationalization powers are in full swing. He is lost, has misplaced the directions and the phone number. No, worse than that. I gave him wrong directions. Of course, it has to be my fault. Marge would say I'm locked in my self-flagellation stage. So, okay, it's not my fault. Maybe he's stuck in traffic caused by a fifty-seven-car pileup. Better yet, maybe he *caused* the fifty-seven-car pileup. That's the only reason good enough for causing me this much distress.

At 7:40, the second glass of wine has not calmed me and I feel a headache building. I reach for the aspirin and flip the lid off on the first try. The unexpected ease of this maneuver causes me to drop the bottle. Aspirin tablets bounce like popcorn in a hundred directions. Annoyed at my clumsiness, I slam the kitchen cabinet door. It slams back at me and disengages from its hinges, bouncing to the floor. Or rather, half of it does. The other half stays on the counter where it bounced first.

I try to focus and regain composure. I'm uncertain of exactly what I feel, whether it's pure rage, pain, or sheer humiliation. I just know some wickedly uncomfortable emotion is batting back and forth in me at such a pace, my heartbeat can't keep up with it. I can't sit, can't stand, can't watch television or read. I try them all at varying intervals for nearly an hour. I can't do anything sane at all, so I call Gordon.

When I hear his voice, my tears break through. "It's okay," he says, in his reassuring tone. "I'll be right over."

Knowing Gordon is on his way calms me somewhat. Gordon is my best friend. A year ago, he and I were married to other people and all of us were friends. We sat together at Little League, squeezed side by side into midget sized school desks at parents' night and chatted casually when one or the other of us was dropping off or picking up a child. His two sons were best friends with my two sons, so all of us were thrown together more often than not. His wife left him for someone Mark's age. (Ugh, awful thought. Remember not to tell Gordon how old my almost date was.) Soon after that, my husband left, and ever since, Gordon and I have huddled together in platonic companionship like the only two puppies left in the pet store window.

When Gordon rings the doorbell, I am wearing my oldest sweatpants and work shirt. These are my comfort clothes. Wrapped in their battered softness, I am beginning to feel a measure of stillness. When I see Gordon's smile, I know I am going to be all right. I still haven't picked up the pretzels, the aspirin or the two pieces of cabinet door.

Without saying a word, Gordon bends to pick up the splintered wood and goes to the closet for a broom and dustpan. "I'll come back tomorrow and fix the door," he says, without even asking me how any of this happened. "But for now, why don't you just sit down and I'll make us some tea."

Over tea we talk about the kids and how much he misses his boys when they're with their mother. We agree to take all four of them to the air show next weekend. "So," he says, smiling his *things are never as bad as they seem* smile "you're gonna be okay, you know. This guy was obviously a jerk. Believe me, you don't know it now, but you're better off that he didn't show up." He gets up and moves toward the window. "Maybe it's too soon for you anyway," he adds, with evident seriousness. "You've got to be strong enough to deal with it. You've still got a lot of bruises to heal."

What he's saying makes sense. So I tell him, as honestly and clearly as I can, that I understand all that but there's a real strong need in me to feel wanted again. To feel someone's eyes move over me like syrup over a pancake. I want to pick up the phone and hear somebody say something besides "Mom,

63

I forgot my lunch money." Just once, I want to have something to look forward to, something special that I'm not responsible for.

He looks at me knowingly and nods. "In time," he says. "And believe me, when you're ready, your phone's gonna be ringing more than you want to hear it. I'm a guy, trust me. I know these things."

"Right. You have to say that, you're my best friend."

"True, but I'm also a guy. And as a guy, I know what guys think. I know what they see. And if we see someone who's just been hurt really bad, we're gonna stay away. Unless of course, we're shmucks, and we want to take advantage of a vulnerable female." He sits across from me and looks me in the eyes. "Forget the date for now," he says, animated. "You want something to look forward to? I'll pick you up tomorrow at six. Whatever you were planning to wear tonight, wear it tomorrow. You can practice your best dating behavior on me. Well, most of it anyway." He plants a kiss on my forehead and goes to the kitchen to gather the cabinet debris. "I'll fix this at home and put it back up tomorrow. Now, get some sleep."

At the door, I reach out and touch his arm. "Thanks," I say. "You've made a miserable night just about enjoyable."

"Well," he says laughing. "That's what best friends are for, right?"

The next morning Marge calls. "I couldn't wait another minute," she says. "I'm dying to know. Was it wonderful?"

"As a matter of fact," I say. "It worked out just fine."

Space Invaders

Just last year, when I looked through the kitchen window in the house I left behind, I was eye-to-eye with a doe who had come down from the woods to breakfast on my variegated Hosta. She stared at me intently, her body poised to spring if I made a move to challenge her, but her eyes were more questioning than fearful. "I know this is your yard," she seemed to say. "But I had a yard once too before suburbia took it. So do you mind if I share some of your space?" I didn't mind sharing the space, though I wished her appetite were less gourmet and that she would have been satisfied with the pachysandra. But for that moment I felt more like the intruder than the landowner, and I was grateful for the privilege of sharing her four acres for the eight years I had lived there. When I sold my house to "right size" my living quarters, I knew I would miss her.

Today, outside my kitchen window a wren swoops down and lands softly on the hydrangea. The leaf beneath it barely flutters as she tucks her wings behind her. She looks directly into the window and seems to meet my gaze. She's wondering if anyone is home, or maybe she's wondering just who these new people are.

Only a short distance behind the wren, leggy forsythia marks the edge of my property. There, a line of tightly clustered elms shields me from my neighbor's view—at least at the second floor level. On both sides of my new home similar boundaries afford me what limited privacy one can expect from a lot just large enough to provide a decorative frame around the foundation of a house. All at once, I am aware of neighbor noise. I hear them closing and opening their car doors, I hear screen doors bang shut. And now that soundless hot summer winds have driven people outside in search of air, I am privy to many more conversations, and often exclamations, than I care to hear. It becomes increasingly clear to me that I am suffering from space invasion.

I know I determined my boundaries long before I acquired four acres of land in rural Connecticut. Perhaps my need for space goes back to the day my sister drew a hostile chalk line on the green carpet in the room we shared, threatening bodily harm if I or any of my personal belongings so much as touched the surface on the other side.

From my side of the chalk line I looked longingly across the expanse to two things I knew I could not live without—the closet and the door. I quickly scanned my somewhat less than half a room to see if I had any bargaining power. There had to be something I could trade for exit and entry privileges. In my panic I decided then and there that I would acquire my own space someday with lots of escapes that could not be commandeered by space invaders. I ended up some years later in a house with six doors that opened to the outside. I was happy with that. This house, however, has only two avenues of escape: the front door and the back door; discounting, of course, the cellar. I pacify myself with the notion that there are also only two easily accessible ways in. There is some security in that rationale. It will have to do.

The kitchen curtains in my new house sway slightly as the warm breeze blows through carrying the excited chatter of the children who live behind me. I can't see them through the hedge that separates us, but since I'm unaccustomed to noise, it sounds like a full cavalry of kids to me. Suddenly a large red ball flies over the leafy green barrier and into the shrub beneath my window. The nesting wren bolts into the air and flies away. I take a deep breath and walk out the door to face the miniature army that would undoubtedly invade my yard to retrieve the ball. Outside, in the middle of my lawn stands a little boy with cropped brown curls. With his hands behind him he tilts his head to one side and says, "Hi, my name is Morgan. Can I have my ball?"

I bend to pick it up and take a few steps toward him. "Of course you can," I say, stopping about four feet away holding the ball out to him.

"Do you know how to play kick ball?" he asks.

"Oh sure, I used to play kick ball all the time when I was your age. But I haven't played in a long time."

"You can play with us sometime if you want," he says quite seriously. "My mom plays sometimes, but she runs real slow, so we always get her out."

"I'd like that, Morgan," I say.

"Cool," he says smiling broadly as he turns and disappears through the hedge. I smile and wave as he goes. Maybe my little space invader is about to become a friend.

"Cool," I say out loud to myself as I walk back in my house and close the door. Glancing out the window, I see the wren has reclaimed her perch. The noise of kick ball resumes to full volume and Frank Sinatra is singing "Summer Wind" in my next door neighbor's living room. "I think I could get used to this," I say to the wren, just as the golden retriever two houses down joins Frank in the final chorus.

Is There Any Place Like Home?

"When are you coming home?" my sister asked when I called yesterday. "I wish I could," I answered, feeling strangely as if I were, in fact, somewhere far from home. I wasn't. I was home. My home. It happens to be nine hundred miles from her home, from my parents, my brother, and the high school that taught me algebra. But it is, nonetheless, where I live—the place where I find solace after a bad day, the place I complain about when the windows need to be washed and the leaves are nearly three feet deep in November. It's the address on my checks, the place where my phone rings if someone is looking for me, but is it home?

Last week when I was in New York, I drove by the house that was once my grandmother's. I stood on the sidewalk and looked up the thirty-two steps that separated me from the front porch. I could almost hear the sound of my footsteps on the gray wood. When I was six, this was my sanctuary. I would walk the three blocks from my house alone and traverse this mammoth incline as fast as I could, never feeling the breathlessness of exertion. Always, as if by magic, my grandmother would know exactly when I would arrive, and she'd be holding the screen door wide for me as I plowed through. Inside, time would stop. It was Friday night, no school tomorrow, no sister declaring herself queen for the day and of the room we shared at home. No little brother competing for attention. Every Friday night was mine.

After tea and cookies, I would dig the Chinese checkers out of the closet and she would let me win twice. A jigsaw puzzle she couldn't seem to finish alone would taunt us from the dining room table. "I can't find the last piece of the moon," she'd say on her way into the kitchen. "See if you can find it." And there it would be, glowing brightly from the middle of dozens of unconnected shapes that would eventually become a forest. "Grandma, I found it!" I'd yell.

"Aren't you clever!" she'd answer. "And there I was half the day looking for it." At night she'd tuck me into her huge four poster bed that seemed as high off the ground as the kitchen table. The sheets were pressed and pulled so tightly across the mattress, I felt as if I were bandaged in. Outside the window, the streetlight threw gold shafts of light between the venetian blinds, and when I closed my eyes, I could still see yellow lines. "Grandma, can you see through your eyelids?" I'd ask her.

"Not without my glasses," she'd say.

When I was seven, my family moved to North Carolina, and I never ran the three blocks from my house to hers on Fridays again. In fact, my grandmother and I saw very little of each other over the remainder of her life. But still, when I think of home, I think of her house—the kitchen table pushed up against the window so she could watch the birds in her garden and bang on the glass if a dreaded blue jay intruded on her beloved wrens. The china hutch in the dining room that housed her mother's teacup collection held all the mystery of a giant treasure chest for me. There was a yellow cup with butterfly wings for a handle, and one with a rose on the inside. Even though they were all she had left of her childhood in England, she let me choose the one I liked best for tea time.

The yellow butterfly cup is now inside my mother's china cabinet. The house my parents call home was built the year I moved out. It never had a room I called mine, and yet my children and I feel its tug when we think of Thanksgiving and Christmas. I've moved twenty times in my life—called twenty places home. My children moved eight times before they took the giant leap to college. And although my mother wasn't crazy about Chinese checkers, my children learned how to add single digit numbers when they were four playing Parcheesi at her dining room table. It's the same table in the same room where she lit birthday candles for my sons on cakes that evolved through the years from Cookie Monster to "just chocolate, please."

The house where I live now has assumed a life of its own. It doesn't remember the thud of my sons' baseball bats being tossed into closets or the melodic sound of Dr. Seuss rhymes at bedtime. Its fireplace served as a backdrop for only one prom picture. In fact, my oldest son moved away two months before I bought this house, and the furniture he left behind has been transformed with wedding ring quilts and embroidered pillows to complement a butter yellow guest room.

Still, there is something of the family's spirit here. On the plate rack in my new kitchen is a dish that once served my mother's deviled eggs. On the wall in the hallway is a watercolor my grandmother painted when she was sixteen—the year before she left England. In my china cabinet is a pottery ashtray my son Bryan made in the second grade. And, until it fell off the wall and broke last month, a wooden plaque studded with black nails and labeled "keys," in Jason's ten-year-old scrawl, hung by the back door.

This year, when we began to talk about holidays, I was afraid some other place would be calling my sons home—that memories of family gatherings would conjure up longings for more familiar ground. Friends of theirs still come home to trophy-lined rooms and backyards appointed with sagging basketball hoops and tree forts. They'll walk across kitchens where they took their first steps and back cars out of the same driveways they sailed down the day their fathers took off the training wheels. Knowing this, I wasn't sure just what my sons thought of when they thought of home.

But today, when the phone rang and I heard my son's voice say once again, "Mom, I can't wait to get there," I knew for sure—there are lots of places like home.

Part Two

One Wrong Turn
Can Lead to Nebraska:
A Daughter's Journey

Nearing the end of my thirties, I decided it was time to get to know my father. When I was a child, he was someone I loved and feared with equal measure. I was quiet in his presence, because it seemed the only sure way to avoid one of his thundering reprimands. As a teenager, I often felt my brother, sister, and I had been corralled rather than reared. My father preferred the electric fence approach to the participatory one. With occasional but sharp vocal reminders of exactly where our boundaries lay, we were free to roam and discover at our own discretion. Once or twice a year we traveled somewhere in a car and spent about fourteen days in another location—usually coastal. We called it the family vacation. For two weeks our boundaries changed, and we were given opportunities to explore and create our own adventures, or not—whatever we chose.

Only recently, I realized my father's expression of love was that gift of freedom. My friends' parents, it seemed, kept them under constant vigil, initiating conversations that felt more like interrogations than exchanges of ideas or feelings. Had they done their homework, practiced the piano, cultivated the appropriate friends in the right families, applied for student council and the yearbook committee? I watched as my friends faced their parents' expectations with either furious determination or abject defiance. Still, there was a part of me that longed for my father's involvement—a firm hand pressed against my back, propelling me forward into achievements I wouldn't have attempted alone. "Why don't you try out for the school play?" I longed to hear. "You'd be great. I'll help you practice after dinner. We'll read from *Oedipus,* because if you can play that, you can play anything."

Instead, our discussions took on the flavor of fishing expeditions. "Dad, I'm thinking about joining the drama club. What do you think?"

"I know you'd be great at anything you try," he'd answer, always. "You just have to want it badly enough to work at it." I didn't recognize it at the time, but my father was offering me the world—a world full of opportunity and challenge. But that wasn't what I wanted. I wanted a world that was easy. A world where anything I desired would be mine without much of a struggle. A bounty of treasure and experience through which he would guide me unscathed, using a map he had charted himself. My father had a different idea. He believed the experience of learning which way to go was better than the journey itself.

"Tell me what to do," I pleaded, two days before my sixth grade science project was due. "I can't think of anything."

"There's no such word as *can't.*" I mouthed the words as he said them. I knew, as soon as I heard myself say it, that this would be his response. Not to be outdone, I countered, "*Can't* is too a word. I've looked it up."

"It's not in *my* dictionary," he said, for the thousandth time, tapping his temple with an index finger. "Yes, you can think of something," he continued. "And, don't ever depend on other people to think for you. You know, if I gave you detailed directions how to get from Atlanta to New York City and gave you one left turn that was a mistake, you'd end up in Nebraska."

"What does that mean?" I moaned, in eleven-year-old exasperation.

"Think about it," he said, leaving little doubt that the discussion had ended.

I won first prize in the science fair that year, but I never understood about the left turn to Nebraska. In fact, I didn't understand very much at all about my father. And until recently, I never thought to ask.

"Dad, do you ever wish your life had been different?"

"If I had the chance to live the same life over again," he said, without hesitation, "I'd take it in an instant."

His answer surprised me. I'm his daughter. I know what he has suffered. Not because he's told me, but because I know enough of his history to know his life couldn't have been easy. The ninth of ten children, my father survived poverty, the depression, the South Pacific during WWII and the loss of most of his family and best friends.

"I'm sure I'd probably make the same mistakes," he said almost wistfully. "You know, those things I said I was doing for the family, when I was really doing them because I wanted the challenge. But then again, maybe I'd know the difference this time."

I knew the things he was talking about. They were decisions that affected all of our lives. Decisions that jolted us from familiar havens and plunged us into strange territory—new schools, new friends, new houses that felt cold and plain. Decisions that pretty much made us who we are today, good or bad. I realized then that this was his way of acknowledging our suffering—his attempt to rectify all the things he might believe he had done. But it was also his way of telling me who he was.

I'd like to say that in that instant I knew him, his strengths, his vulnerabilities, what made him happy. Instead, in that instant I knew myself. I recognized the voice inside my head that says "You can do this," when I know my own voice is saying, "This is too hard." Every time I get discouraged, and I think a dream is too big, or a question unanswerable, I hear him say, "Think about it." That's when I know the discussion has ended, and the next move is mine.

Playing the Jack of Hearts

When the curtain finally rises, I realize I'm holding my breath. I see feet first—a rainbow of sneakers, and then bulbous knees. Probably, although I can't quite see, most of those knees bear battle scars of this week's playground activities. I know for a fact that at least one of those knees has a big blue bruise exactly the size of the toe on an eight-year-old's soccer shoe. Although I don't readily recognize the set of knees that belongs to my son, I'm reasonably certain he's the third one from the left. I know that only because I've watched this scene before without the suspenseful introduction of a curtain lifting. In fact, I've watched this scene so many times, I could play all the parts. This play has had more rehearsals than *42nd Street*, and by now, every mother in the audience is poised on the edge of her chair prepared to mouth every line, as if telepathically we could guarantee that no child would be struck dumb by stage fright.

My son is the Jack of Hearts in *Alice in Wonderland*. My neighbor's son, Matthew, is the White Rabbit. Jason said he didn't really want that part anyway, but his tone was not convincing. I told him not to take it personally, because the lead always went to the child whose mother could make the best costume. While my limited talent was helpful in copying the Jack of Hearts onto poster board, I would be paralyzed transforming ten yards of white felt into a walking, talking rabbit. He seemed pleased with that explanation, although twenty years from now he may blame me for his failed acting career. *I could have been a great dramatic actor if only my mother had learned to sew.*

The audience is applauding now. The heavy maroon curtain has ascended into the rafters and twenty-five faces gleaming beneath hastily combed or carefully ponytailed hair gaze—some unconsciously, others nervously—at the audience. I can tell from the intent stare that my son is looking for me. Don't look, I'm thinking. Just remember your lines. I guess at this moment I'm the typical stage mother. And probably, just like the other mothers in the audience, I'm feeling my son's heartbeat from here.

"What if I forget what to say?" he asked, more than once.

"You won't," I answered, trying to reassure him, but afraid to promise him something I wasn't absolutely sure of. "But if you feel like you are, just look over at Mrs. Baker. She has it all written down and she'll be standing just past the curtain." He turned and looked to the right. We were in our kitchen, not the auditorium, but practicing the gesture seemed to reassure him. "Do you really think my costume will be okay, Mom?" he asked. Then, realizing his question signaled doubt about my artistic capabilities, he tensed his shoulders and changed his approach. "I mean, are you sure we bought the right kind of paint?"

"I'm sure," I said smiling at the thought of him protecting my feelings. Clearly, his concern about fitting in with the rest of the playing deck should take precedence over my fragile artist's ego. "We bought the paint Mrs. Baker told us to buy, and we used her stencil. So, we can't miss. It will be perfect."

And it is, because it is, in fact, our third try. My first Jack of Hearts leaned lazily to the left. When Jason put it on and walked to the mirror, he anchored his arms to his side and leaned to the right. "It's great Mom. Thanks," he said stoically.

"Sure it is," I said, pulling it over his head and tossing it aside. "If your right leg is five inches shorter than your left one." My second Jack was straight, but he was also demonic. We must have stood him up before he was quite dry. His eyes narrowed into a sadistic leer and his mouth twisted down at the edge,

80

giving him an evil scowl that was sure to frighten the Dormouse, little Amy Bracken. On our third trip to town for poster board, we developed a strategy. "You know, Mom," Jason began. "If we got some tape, maybe we could tape the stencil to the poster so it wouldn't move when you paint over it." The white rabbit's mother probably would have thought of that, which is why she's moved on to white felt, and I'm still in poster board.

The croquet match is the only scene Jason is in, and this play is his first experience in front of a large audience. The only thing he knows about being nervous is that people make fun of other people who make mistakes. And Jason clearly does not want to be made fun of. At the tender age of eight, fear of humiliation has far surpassed fear of the dark or monsters in the closet. "I can't wear that shirt, Mom," he will say of the same shirt he couldn't live without six months ago. "It's geeky." The mere fact that he's willing to risk his reputation by appearing on stage in a costume he trusted me to create is almost more pressure than I can endure.

When he enters the stage, the Ace, Two, and Three of Clubs are painting the white roses red for the Queen of Hearts. The Clubs mistakenly planted white roses, instead of the red ones ordered by the Queen and now are frantically trying to cover their mistake as the Queen enters the garden. Alice, played by Marie Berringer, whose mother owns the local flower shop, is joining the Clubs in a chorus of "Every way is the Queen's way, so we're painting the roses red," when they're all caught red-handed (so to speak) by the Queen. Just then, Jason steps forward to pronounce his one and only line. "Someone will lose his head over this." But there's no sound. He stops and looks toward the audience. The Queen, Alice, and all of the Clubs turn to look at him. His eyes grow round and large, or maybe I just imagine that because I know his eyes get large when he gets frightened or confused. Then he turns hesitantly to the right, where he knows Mrs. Baker is standing. Magically, it all comes back to him. He lifts his spear over his head and shouts with conviction, "Somebody's head's gonna roll for this!" Laughter fills the auditorium.

In the car on the way home he announces that he's retiring from the theater. "Why?" I ask in amazement. "You were great."

81

"No, I wasn't," he replies, looking down at his lap where he's holding the Jack of Hearts now folded awkwardly and permanently into an eight inch square. "I didn't say it the way I was supposed to. Marie said I was stupid if I couldn't remember one dumb line, and that I ruined it for everybody." Now that the words are out, so are the tears. I hate times like this, when every self-help parenting book fails you. I hate this moment especially, because I realize that up till now, I pretty much had agreed with Marie. I had even gone so far as to prepare a speech in my head about concentration, being prepared, paying attention and not letting other people down. I was just waiting for the right moment to begin.

Instead, I take a deep breath and pull the car to the side of the road. Holding his face in my hands I look into his eyes and push tears aside with my thumbs. "Marie's just jealous," I say, "because you stole the show from her. In one perfectly timed moment you captured an entire audience." I feel the muscles in his cheeks begin to relax and I know he's aching to believe me. "What you have, Jason, is style under pressure," I continue, feeling for the first time that I really am telling the truth. "You know what that is? That's star quality." I kiss him lightly on the cheek, then ease the car back onto the road. "You have real star quality."

"You really think so, Mom?" he asks, the lightness returning to his voice.

"Yes, Jason. I really think so."

The rest of the ride home we sing, "We're painting the roses red. We're painting the roses red. Every way is the Queen's way, so we're painting the roses red."

Cobwebs and Other Hazards of Self-Employment

I decided it was time to get serious about my career. I also decided in order to do that, I needed someone else to get serious about keeping my house clean. For some reason, every time I sit down to map out my future or devise a strategy for my career advancement, the only vision I can conjure up is one of three thousand giant dust balls gathering strength under the furniture.

Working at home as a freelance public relations consultant, I find myself alone in a house that is screaming for order. Unlike the rest of the household, I can't walk out and forget it from nine to five. To get to my desk, I have to cross through the kitchen and extract my eyeglasses from beneath a pile of yesterday's newspapers. Beside it is an equally obtrusive stack of oatmeal bowls. Moments from now, their contents will have cemented them together permanently.

Clearing the breakfast table commits me to thirty minutes, give or take a few, in the kitchen. I reason a load of laundry may as well be in process while the dishes soak. Still moving in the direction of my desk, now with a load of towels to deposit in the washing machine, I realize I'm following a distinct trail of cookie crumbs that connects the kitchen to the couch in the den. To vacuum the rug should take no more than ten minutes. However, perched in the middle of the otherwise open expanse is a mammoth spaceship composed of building blocks the size of fingernails. Moving it is dangerous. Not because of its apparent value to the seven-year-old who designed it, but because of its potential to self-destruct into twenty million pieces that would have to be retrieved without the aid of electric devices.

Carefully, and cleverly, I slide the flattened lid of a cardboard box under the spacecraft. And instantly, as if struck by a lethal laser from a warring planet, it disintegrates. I picture the look of utter horror I will see on Bryan's face this afternoon and make a few vain attempts to reconstruct it. But in the end, I spend more time picking up the fifteen million pieces that didn't land in the box. I make a mental note to turn this experience into a story with a moral by the time he gets home.

Once the rug is crumb and track free, the laundry spinning joyfully, and the spaceship properly recycled, I know I better avoid the upstairs altogether if there's any hope of ever getting to my desk today.

By now, most of the nation's work force is on their first official coffee break of the day, and I have yet to even switch on my computer. In less than three hours, the doors will burst open and I'll hear, "Mom, I'm home!" followed almost immediately by, "I can't find my _____ ball." Either basket, base, soccer or Nerf. He has it down to a science. The only one that's not clearly visible is the one he wants.

I think of Mrs. Fields and Mary Kay and I am awed—no, more than that—cowed, by their success. Who cleaned the bathrooms before Mrs. Fields sold her first cookie? Clearly, I had to either let it go or get someone else to do it.

"I get twenty dollars an hour, a fifty-dollar minimum. I could squeeze you in Tuesday mornings between 11:30 and 1:00," says a woman on the phone who was described in her classified ad as "thorough, reasonable, and insured." Busy and expensive is usually a good sign with hair stylists. Perhaps the same holds true with housekeepers. Based on what I know I will get paid for the project I'm working on, I think I can afford Ms. Reasonable maybe twice a month. It will have to do.

I think I half expected a Carol Burnett figure with buckets and mops wielding a half-dozen spray bottles. To work that fast, she must have some magic formula for cleaning shower tiles. I begin to get excited about the prospect of dust-free baseboards and a chandelier that isn't draped with strands of cobwebs.

Imagine having both bathrooms clean at the same time, being able to fill the tub with bath salts and hot water without having to scrub the ring away first.

The day Janine comes (wielding only a set of car keys) I point her in the direction of the cleaning equipment and settle in front of my computer. I delight in the distant sound of a roaring vacuum cleaner. Seemingly only moments later a voice calls down the hallway. "I'm finished."

Even though only an hour and forty-five minutes have actually passed, as per her requirements she receives the full fifty dollars. "You're leaving so soon?" I ask.

"It's an easy house," she says. "You being home all day, I guess, you keep it pretty tidy. Wasn't much to it at all."

Closing the door behind her, I notice a thin fog of dust rise from the surface of the baseboard heater in the hallway. Passing through the kitchen, my foot sticks in the spot where Jason spilled his juice that morning. I guess I forgot to mention the floor should be washed. In the den, I run my hand over the tables and television. They're clean. I check the shelves, one, two . . . perhaps she wasn't tall enough to reach the top two.

As I continue my inspection of furniture surfaces, I discover a random sampling of untouched places. Mostly, there's no logical pattern for the omissions. In one bedroom, a nightstand nearly bows under the weight of a thick layer of dust, while another fairly glows with a new wax shine. In the bathrooms, mirrors sparkle, but the sinks are ringed and dull. The dining room table boasts a satin sheen, but the floor plays host to an army of dust balls hiding under the table's pedestal.

All in all, the house looks pretty much like it does on the days my friend Bert calls and says she's stopping by for lunch. I rush around madly picking things up and shining anything chrome plated she is likely to encounter. In fact, I realize I had done exactly that this morning before Janine arrived. I had thought it best not to overwhelm her on her first day.

I decide not to invite Janine back. Instead, I will pay myself every Monday: $15 an hour to clean the house the way I know it should be done. Then, I'll dedicate the rest of the week to my real work.

85

Monday evening, I'm exhausted after my first full day as my own housekeeper and I collapse into the sofa. Tomorrow I will ignore it all, I tell myself. I'll toss the breakfast dishes into the sink and devote the day to work. Delighted with my new scheme I yell to the boys to start their baths. "And don't mess up the bathroom!" I add for emphasis.

"Come on Mom," my oldest whines. "Why can't we stay up? We don't have school tomorrow. It's teacher's conference. Remember? You said we could go to the go-cart track."

Oh well, I think, as I drop my head back and roll my eyes to the ceiling. I guess my career can wait one more day. Out of the corner of my eye, I see a faint gray shape. I turn to focus and see a gracefully arching cobweb dangling like a fairy's wing from the recessed light in the ceiling just above my head. It sways gently as I exhale a heavy sigh. I wonder: What are cobs anyway and why is it no one ever catches them spinning their webs?

86

 Political Leanings

At age fourteen, my son, a self-proclaimed, right-wing conservative, sat stone-faced through the Republican National Convention. Not because he's interested in the candidate's views on foreign policy, human rights or natural resources, but because he wants to know if taxes and the Dow Jones average are going up.

I have no room to criticize. I didn't watch it at all. I am touched that his concern for my tax bill would prompt him to sacrifice *Star Trek* in the interest of the family's financial security. I realized, however, when he signed his name to a letter, "Registered Republican," that his political concerns extended beyond curiosity.

"What makes you think you are a Republican?" I ask, masking amusement.

"I don't want to pay taxes."

"Republicans are not tax exempt."

"I know, that's the problem," he says. "If I have to pay 30 percent of my income in taxes, how will I afford a BMW? They say Democrats will raise taxes and give all the money away. In that case, I will have to be Republican."

At this point I realize argument is futile. I am basically apolitical and the phantom "they," to whom all adolescents so quickly allude, is all-knowing and all-powerful, a force with which I am unprepared to reckon.

Today when I get home I notice he is reading *U.S. News and World Report.* In my excitement at seeing him using his optic nerves on something unrelated to television, I am slow to comprehend the implications.

Jason, who just last year thought Richard Nixon had been a Democrat and that Johannesburg was a cheese casserole, spent two dollars of his hard-earned lawn-mowing money to purchase a news magazine. I am, for a brief moment, quite impressed.

I look closer and see that his attention is riveted to an article on Donald Trump.

"Check out this yacht, Mom. Wouldn't you like to have that kind of money?"

"Actually, no," I answer. "The more you have, the more you have to worry about it. I wouldn't want more than I'd have time to spend."

I am treading close to my dreaded materialism sermon here and he knows it. It starts the same way every time.

"Yeah, yeah, I know," he groans. "Money can't buy me happiness."

It occurs to me that my surprise, and in turn, my displeasure over his preoccupation with materialism boarders on hypocrisy. He is wearing a polo player on his chest and shoes that are purportedly pumped with air. It's blatant commercialism I fell for. Maybe out of some sense of belonging I hoped to provide for him. In any case, these lapses are holdovers from more affluent times, more extravagant gift giving. Today, on a single mother's budget, I tend to view those branding strategies as consumer fraud and try to communicate that sentiment to my children. However, I'm beginning to see that I am making no headway. Perhaps because they see it as a philosophy recently adopted from my circumstances, not my convictions.

All that aside, why he has confused party affiliations and politics with country club memberships and personal finance, I cannot fathom. But he seems convinced that a four bedroom house and BMW are the Republican administration's equivalent to forty acres and a mule. He foresees golf as the national pastime and Alaskan king crab legs as the staple of the American family.

"By the way, Mom. About that fifty dollars you borrowed: You don't have to pay it back."

All is not lost, I think. There is some compassion left. Some concern for the less fortunate. Perhaps he noted the disapproval in my voice and was duly chastised. I feel compelled to push the issue.

"Thanks," I say. "But don't you think that's a big risk, giving money away? I may lose my incentive to work."

"Yeah, I know," he says, smiling. "But I need the practice. Some day I'll get to claim deductions for charitable contributions."

# A Place to Hide

For fourteen years now I have lived in a household with children. These children occupy no less than 99 percent of the house. The remaining 1 percent, which remains thus far undefiled by my offspring's intrusion, is the inside of the dishwasher. If I could fit, that is where I would hide when I think I can't stand one more minute of: "Mom, I hate my brother. Will you make him go live with Dad?" "Mom, Mrs. Bachman gave me detention because Craig was talking," or "Jeez, Mom, I put that shirt in the wash yesterday. I thought I could wear it for class pictures today."

The dishwasher is safe, I know. Because my children do not know it opens.

When I was a child, the mothers I knew established their own personal places of refuge. My friend Kathy's mother had rooms in her house with unseen yet forbidding "no trespassing signs." In those rooms were treasured antiques with hand-rubbed finishes and silk damask upholstery. At least, that's what I heard, I never actually went in them. Once Kathy glanced into the living room from the foyer and saw her mother stretched out on the blue brocade Louis XV settee. She quickly dashed for a flashlight in the hall closet and shined it in her mother's face. "Excuse me, Madame," Kathy said clearing her throat in her best security guard imitation while pretending to unhook an imaginary velvet rope from the door frame. "The museum is closing now and you'll have to leave."

I suppose Kathy's mother thought it was worth the risk of sagging cushions and napped fabric to capture a few stolen moments of peace away from her five children and their friends. In fact, the imaginary velvet ropes that kept the children at bay were probably designed to preserve her sanctuary rather than ward off furniture scars and carpet tracks. In any event, the concept worked on both counts.

My mother, on the other hand, was a proponent of the "lived in" look. "If you can't use it," she was fond of preaching, "you shouldn't own it." So there were no rooms reserved for adult guests only. Still, she also believed in establishing a forbidden territory to which she could retreat unfollowed. It was her bedroom. That room was, she insisted, the only patch of earth she could claim as her own, and she was not willing to share it with her children. We were certain she had installed highly sophisticated tracking devices to protect her domain, because she always knew when one of us had been in there to use the phone. I have since discovered her simple secret of detection—one that children would never suspect: Bedspreads wrinkle when sat upon.

My bedroom is not protected by a child exclusion designation. That's where my children find me when they feel like talking. When my fourteen-year-old was a toddler and barely tall enough to climb up on my bed unassisted, he would pull my book from my hands and replace it with Dr. Seuss' *Cat in the Hat* or *Sneeches*. There we would huddle together for an hour or more reading, talking, or playing "guess my number."

Now, the reading material has changed (term papers and report cards), but my room is, more than ever, the place where souls unburden, encouragement soothes, and anger unleashes. Almost daily one of them will find me hiding with the latest *House Beautiful* or stack of papers. He'll sit on my bed and begin with, "Don't get mad, Mom," or "Don't say anything yet," and sometimes "You're gonna love this, Mom." (Usually, I don't.) And so it begins. The conversations flow like an uncharted river, turning up wherever there's a channel.

I'm glad about that, and I wouldn't want to dampen that open atmosphere. But that leaves me with no place to hide. Even my bathroom is not secure enough. I have a huge bathtub where I have sought refuge many over-stressed evenings. My children, who are old enough to knock before bursting through the bathroom door, are, however, quite adept at creatively circumventing protocol.

Just recently my water-based meditation was interrupted by a knock. "What do you want?" I shouted above the sound of running water. My reply was interpreted as permission. The door opened a crack. A whirring sound followed, and through the door rolled a radio-controlled red Volkswagen pulling a trailer made of Legos. "Tell me if it gets stuck," said a pleased-with-himself voice behind the door. The car navigated successfully to the tub and stopped. Behind the car, sitting atop the makeshift flatbed, was a large blue mug of hot tea. I was far too impressed with the innovation and touched by the gesture to get angry.

I am beginning to think my children are inescapable. Maybe they're not like everyone else's. They have built-in radar sensors and powers that enable them to do impossible things. For instance, they can perform molecular transference from the distant corners of the house to appear instantly before me if I pick up the phone to call my friend or open a carton of ice cream. On the other hand, if I call them to set the table or empty the dryer they vanish with equal quickness. When these powers first surfaced, I thought they were only temporary—that age and maturity would diminish their intensity. But so far, nothing has changed but their height and their voices.

In the waiting, I have fled like a nomad from refuge to refuge—stealing and hoarding moments of solace like treasured relics. Tonight I will go home and announce, "what a great night to clean the basement!" In a puff of smoke they will vanish to the uppermost reaches of the house and I will savor at least an hour of uninterrupted silence.

93

Nightmare in the Making

"Can I be Freddy for Halloween?" my son asks.

"Freddy who?" I ask back, thinking none of the Freds I ever knew were popular enough to warrant a costumed imitation.

"Oh Mom! You know. Freddy Krueger—*Nightmare on Elm Street.*"

"What?" I scream, turning pan-in-hand from the stove so quickly my sautéed asparagus spears soar like tiny green ski jumpers across the kitchen. "You want to dress up as a psychopathic madman who tortures and murders children? Have you lost your mind?"

My heart is pounding. I have purposely forbidden my children to watch R-rated movies, especially those that depend on blood and gore to disguise the absence of plot. Despite my diligence, my son has somehow managed to get himself possessed by this feared demon. Perhaps my response is a bit dramatic, slightly reactive. But I picture my son as the member of some perverse cult—hundreds of Freddy Kruegers with clawed gloves chanting around a fire in the woods.

Bryan is clearly confused by the look of horror on my face. "Come on, Mom, you're supposed to dress up like somebody scary for Halloween. Who do you think I should be, Moses?"

Actually, that wouldn't be a bad idea, but I realize he is merely attempting sarcasm. He's rolling his eyes and shaking his head. He's pretty sure it's time for my lecture on "what we think about we bring about," or even better, "if you lie down with dogs . . ." well, you know. I never knew how that one ended, but I've gotten a good deal of mileage out of it anyway. It's pretty clear he wants none of this and he's backing away.

"Okay, let's think about this," I say, afraid of losing my audience and missing a prime opportunity to punctuate the story with a moral. "You have never been allowed to watch those movies and you know why."

"Right. Because you think if I watch them I'll want to be an ax murderer when I grow up. Because I'll think that hacking off people's arms and legs is really cool. But really, Mom, you don't have to worry about that. There's not enough money in ax murdering. I'd rather be a rock star."

It's a clever argument, and I'm almost swayed. Much too logical for a twelve-year-old. "No, I'm not worried about your career choice," I say, wondering if I'm even convincing myself anymore.

I've fought this battle for years, since the invention of VCRs. Before that, I could simply tell Bryan and his older brother they couldn't go to the movies. These days, families bring this stuff home and pump it out of the television. I have no control at other houses, and because of that, I have much less control over what my children experience. It's a hard battle to wage alone, and while there is no evidence to support me, I still believe that continually exposing my children to the obscene violence, the abhorrent evil, and worse, the senseless torture that these movies glorify, is slowly chipping away at their sensitivity.

"I'm worried that you'll become desensitized to pain and suffering, and that you'll come to believe violence is a reasonable solution to problems." His nose scrunches and his eyes cross. I'm not getting through to him and I can understand why. I'm confusing myself. How do I explain in words what to me is nothing more than a nagging intangible fear? I know in my heart that young children should not be encouraged to relate to or identify with horrific, loathsome creatures. But then again, Dracula has been a welcome guest at most Halloween parties I've attended. Is there a difference? Maybe not.

My son has always read me well and takes the opportunity to play on my doubts. "But what about Frankenstein, Mom? And the Mummy. They killed people and everyone dresses up like them. I don't understand why Freddy is any different."

I don't know how to answer that. I always pictured those mythical creatures as misunderstood misfits who hurt people accidentally or in self-defense. Perhaps I don't know my monsters as well as I should. I realize that in this arena I cannot make a rational, informed decision and cannot pretend to know what I do not.

There is no choice, therefore, but to settle this dispute in the traditional manner. When there is no rhyme or reason, no license or logic, there is one answer that serves all situations.

"Because I said so."

"Okay, Mom," he says with a shrug, giving up far too easily. "Then I'll be Larry Bird. Can you make me a Celtics warm-up jacket and pants? I need them for Bethany's party Friday." He pulls a *Sports Illustrated* from behind his back and slides it across the kitchen counter. "See? They look like this. Remember the Batman costume you made me a long time ago? This would be much easier, wouldn't it?"

He picks up his basketball from under the coffee table, where it rests between games, and bounces it down the hallway. Opening the door to the front yard, he turns and smiles. "You know, Mom, you're right about Freddy. He's really gross."

The door closes. I study the picture of Larry Bird bedecked in kelly green satin and wonder where in the world they sell that material. Next year, I tell myself, I'll let the monster win.

By the Book

It looked so easy when I was a child. Mothers were the women who knew everything, could do everything, and never cried or slept. They were there when you woke up and when you came home. They made buttercream frosting and poured orange soda at birthday parties, sat through *Bambi* and *Old Yeller*, and sewed imitation Chanel suits from Butterick patterns.

Mothers had the potatoes and chicken on the table at the same time and never had to get up for the salt. And three days a week, in the steamy summers, they packed peanut butter sandwiches and grape juice, blew up beach toys, and drove you and your friends to the lake.

So, once in a while, when my mother stamped and fumed and hurled threats like, "I can't wait until you have your own house so I can come and put my feet on your table and leave my crayons all over your rug," I was more amused than frightened. After all, that's what mothers were made for, polishing furniture and picking up crayons.

Now that I have two scratched coffee tables of my own and have picked up and thrown away more crayons than I care to count, I find I am often challenged to redefine "motherhood." Through some unpredictable error of fate, I am unable, and perhaps a little unwilling, to fit into my mother's mold.

After producing no fewer than eight Thanksgiving dinners, I still can't make gravy without lumps. I rarely remembered to give my children their vitamins or fluoride rinse. My oldest son often brought me tea in bed after he had found his own breakfast, and my youngest traditionally opted for pizza and a movie for his birthday, because he knows I despise parties.

They laugh when they find forgotten baked potatoes cold and wrinkled in the toaster oven. And many cold winter mornings they can be found downstairs scrounging through laundry that has not yet made its way upstairs into drawers.

My mother doesn't put her feet on my table or scatter crayons on my floor when she comes to visit. Instead, she manages to get the fish and the noodles to the table while they're still hot. And while she's here, my children forget how to pour their own milk and make their beds, but remember to brush their teeth and comb their hair.

When she's here they no longer think washing a load of clothes for me is a fair exchange for a game of catch. Grandma does all the laundry (even retrieves it from under beds and turns it right side out) and still plays five games of "Crazy Eights" before dinner.

After she's gone, and they are lazing in the remnants of their pampered fiefdom, I begin to wonder if I am, in fact, depriving my children of a nurturing that is crucial to their development. The days string together with my ravings and sermons about responsibility and teamwork, and I wonder if my children will be traumatized for life because they have to change their own sheets and empty the dishwasher.

Admittedly, single mother's guilt plays a large part in this prophesied doom. I live in the shadow of PTA presidents who volunteer as school library aides and class mothers who bake four hundred cupcakes for the Cub Scout Rally. Realistically, when I'm trying not to beat myself up, I'm reasonably sure my sons are content knowing they won't run into me in the hallways at school while they are strutting their stuff.

I also know that by insisting they learn and perform the mechanics of domestic survival I am providing a great service to the future of this country, more specifically, to two prospective brides.

Still, in sweet irony, I often hear myself spouting my mother's monologues in my efforts to achieve this end.

"Just wait until you get your own house," I berate my son, who is sitting with his feet on the table holding two halves of an Oreo only inches from my new couch. "I'm going to come and drop cookie crumbs all over your carpet." He is as threatened by this as I was at his age and doesn't try to hide his smile.

Minutes later I hear the vacuum cleaner roar to life and a voice shouting above the din, "Hey Mom, when I finish vacuuming you want to shoot some baskets?"

"Sure," I answer. "As soon as your brother finishes the dishes."

Two Outs with
the Bases Loaded

I wish I didn't care if my son were the worst baseball player on his team. I wish I didn't hold my breath and hear my heart pound every time he stepped up to the plate. I wish I didn't find myself praying that the boy in front of him would strike out so that my son wouldn't face the pitcher with two outs and the bases loaded. I wish I could have smiled and shrugged my shoulders when the bat flew through the air striking nothing but red dust blowing in the breeze. But with every hit that wasn't came a crushing blow—to his ego and to my heart.

On the way home he'd sit beside me in somber silence. His first baseball season was nearly over, and he had yet to hit the ball more than six inches beyond the catcher's reach. He turned away to look out the window, and I could see a tear carving a clean line through the dust that covered his face. I felt the pain as much as he did, but was it his pride or mine inflicting it?

I can't ignore that recurring twinge of envy I feel each year as I watch other mothers walk away from the awards ceremonies clutching their son's trophies like queens wielding their scepters. I can't even deny an ignoble prick of embarrassment when I answered a Little League mother, "No, my Jason is the one on the bench, not the pitcher's mound."

My youngest son fared no better in his first chosen sport. It wasn't that he was the worst player on the team, he simply didn't play at all. Week after week he stood there in the middle of the soccer field and watched the ball go by in a mass of tangled feet and legs.

I wanted to help develop their skills and increase their confidence, but there seemed to be nothing I could do. When I tried pitching to my son, the only skill he developed was ball dodging. When I tried soccer, I sadly resembled a trained seal trying to dance on a beach ball.

"Keep working at it boys," I'd mutter in retreat. "And someday . . ."

Someday carried me into seven years of baseball, three of soccer, and, so far, one of basketball. The other non-gifted players had long since left the turf and taken up trumpet lessons or computer clubs. My sons, however, year after year, bounded through the door brandishing baseball sign-up sheets like triumphant flags. And year after year, they filled in the forms with renewed enthusiasm issuing proclamations of impending greatness.

Six days a week I chauffeured my two ballplayers to various fields, and three days a week I sat and watched them engage in competition. With fingers crossed and jaw set, I scarcely took a breath until the last out, inning, or quarter.

I wish I could say it never bothered me to see them spend much of their energy shuffling their feet in the dirt under the benches. I'd like to say I rushed to greet them with shouts of praise and pride at the end of every game regardless of their performance.

The real truth is, I would have given anything to see just one home run—to watch Jason's teammates engulf him as he crossed home plate, slapping high-fives on the way to the dugout. I would have loved to see, just once, the flush of pride on his face when he looked for me in the crowded stands—just once to see him glowing in the glory of his peers.

Even though I wanted these things for my children, and yes, for myself, I wonder sometimes if there would have been a trade-off. Would one day of stardom be enough? Would they then have set unrealistic goals for themselves and found failure intolerable? Would they push and push until they became winners, and would I want to live with two glory-mad egotists?

As it is, I love my sons. I always will. But I also like them—a lot. They are kind, sensitive, affectionate, usually patient, and supportive. Would stardom prove toxic to their temperaments?

Would they begin to chastise others of lesser ability as they were chastised? Would they become one of those bad-tempered, bat-throwing, ground-stomping perfectionists—the kind I feel like drop-kicking out of my yard at birthday parties?

I know if it came to choosing, I'd gladly trade that dream home run just to hear Jason say one more time, "Don't worry about it Mike; you'll get it next time," when his friend unexpectedly strikes out. Because I know that one moment of empathy will do us all more good than a hundred home runs with the bases loaded.

Nevertheless, tomorrow, when number thirty stands at the plate, his bat poised in the air, I will be whispering through clenched teeth, "Please Lord, just one hit . . ."

"What price glory?" For an instant, I forget.

105

Sense and Sensitivity

There it was in black and white. Twelve names. I counted them twice. Even though I wasn't sure how many people were supposed to be on a basketball team, I knew the list was complete. Just as I knew every name on it was the wrong name. Two hundred miles away, my twelve-year-old son was sitting by the phone instead of racing down Okemo Mountain with his brother and step-brother. The longer I stood there counting, the longer he sat by the phone waiting. Reading the list for the third time, I felt as if the sidewalk were falling away beneath my feet. My eyes were stinging with the tears I knew my son would be shedding an hour from now, when I told him he hadn't made the team.

He hadn't wanted to go on the ski trip with his father, because he didn't want to miss this moment on Friday afternoon. "I'll go check the list on my way home," I assured him. "There's no reason to miss the whole weekend." So there I was, standing in the deserted schoolyard, chewing my knuckles and shaking my head wishing I had to do anything else in the world but call my son with this news.

Everywhere Bryan went, his basketball accompanied him. In the car he held it in his lap. Walking to the car he bounced it between his legs. On the way to the mailbox, he bounced it behind his back. He spun it on the tip of his finger and rolled it from the top of one hand, down his arm and around his neck to the other hand. Night after night he stood beneath the basketball hoop in the back yard, dribbling with as much control as rocky Connecticut dirt would allow. The quartz light we nailed to a nearby oak tree carved a blazing circle into the dark woods that surrounded him. From 50 yards away where I stood at the kitchen window, I could see his breath in the cold night trailing behind him as he moved. Hour after hour, his slight five-foot body cast an ominous seven-foot shadow that guarded his every move, creating an opponent Bryan was determined to outmaneuver.

"Who won tonight?" I'd ask when he came in.

"Shaq won," he'd answer shrugging. "I just couldn't shake him tonight." It was our daily ritual.

I memorized the list. Not because I wanted to know who had made the team, but because I had read it so many times it was emblazoned in my memory. On the way home I cursed everyone remotely responsible for the introduction of organized sports into the public school system and rehearsed my conversation with Bryan. I did not want to do this on the phone. I wanted him near me. I wanted to be able to wrap my arms around him and wipe the tears from his cheeks. If I couldn't protect him from pain, I wanted to control its measure. But more than anything else, I wanted to grab the basketball coach by the throat and let him fight for breath while I explained the fragility of a twelve-year-old's ego. Somehow, I wanted him to feel the helpless anguish a mother feels when she sees the agony of rejection in the once hopeful eyes of a young boy who has already endured more disappointments than he was prepared for.

But the truth is, by the time I got home, I knew why Bryan's name wasn't on that list. During the twenty-minute drive to my house, all of my memories of Bryan's childhood flooded the car—hundreds of tender moments brought to life by my sympathy for him. But they also brought to bear evidence that supported the coach's verdict. For the past six months I had witnessed Bryan's athletic skills against an imaginary opponent. I had seen him master trajectory, executing a perfect arc from any given point in the shooting hemisphere. I had seen him fake, dodge, aim, and sink with incredible dexterity and accuracy continually and consistently. But I had seen him do it alone.

What I had never seen in Bryan was a fierce competitive spirit. This was my son—the child that crawled into my lap the day he left for his ski trip. Wrapping his arms around my neck he looked into my eyes and asked, "Do you want me to stay home? I don't want you to be all by yourself." This was the child that always offered me half of his candy bar, the one he pedaled two miles on his bicycle to buy with his own money. The child that offered to trade his favorite shirt to his brother because his brother liked blue better than the yellow one he got for his birthday. The child that could see sadness in my eyes from across the room. "Mom," he'd plead, curling up beside me on the couch, "don't be sad. Let's play 'Crazy Eights.'" The same child that couldn't sit through a Hallmark commercial without embarrassing himself with tears. The same child that gave away his entire set of Star Wars figures because someone had asked for them. This was the boy who was expected to go out on that basketball court and fight for possession of an orange rubber sphere. The very idea was ludicrous.

Still, I was no closer to knowing what to say to him. How do you tell a twelve-year-old he doesn't have the stuff stars are made of? How do you tell him that his is a kind and gentle spirit designed for giving, not taking—for supplying encouragement and support, not demanding attention. How do you tell him you'd rather keep him the way he is, that some day he would fully understand his value in the universe?

He answered the phone in less than half a ring. "Bryan. Hi. How are you?"

"Mom."

He knew.

"I didn't make it, did I?" My throat ached. My hands shook. I would not be able to finish this. He was alone in an unfamiliar condo two hundred miles away. I knew him. I knew his voice. I knew he was clenching his fists and that his eyes were brimming.

"No, Bryan. I'm really sorry . . ."

"Did Derrick make it?"

"Yes, he did." I tried not to let the anger tinge my voice. I tried not to picture little obnoxious Derrick hacking off my prize tulips with his baseball bat.

"Good," Bryan said, almost whispering. "He really did good at try-outs."

"Bryan," I started, "I wish . . ."

"I'm okay, Mom." I wanted to say a thousand things, none of which would have done any good. "Really. It's okay, Mom. Dad will be back soon and we're going out to eat. And Mom, thanks for doing that for me. I'll see you Sunday."

When I hung up the phone I knew instinctively a change was taking place. I had heard something new in his voice—an unfamiliar edge. At that moment I knew with certainty that Bryan's name would be on that list next year, because in that awkward moment I heard his unspoken pledge to himself to become a Derrick. For a time I sat unmoving, revisiting the moments with him I had cherished most—recalling the feel of his eyelashes on my cheek as he gave me a butterfly kiss. I could hear the sound of wonder in his voice when I discovered him sitting droopy-eyed and drowsy on the deck at 5 A.M. waiting to see a sunrise. I wanted to call him back and plead with him not to change, to convince him the price of adolescent sports acclaim was too high for me to pay. I didn't. Instead, I let a wave of sadness wash over me, held it for a moment, and let it go.

110

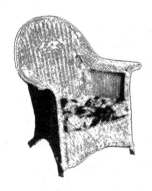

Time Travel: When My Past Meets My Present

During the week, it masquerades as a driving range. Hour after hour, the rocky field endures the repeated smack of hard white balls upon its face. A gutted hillside in southern Connecticut, it stands out like a blistering sore in the midst of the lush verdure that otherwise paints this region.

Here, the land is barren and cragged, naked save for a large sign at the crest of the basin boasting "250 Yards." It seems to taunt would-be golfers, "Hit me if you can." There are few who can, and there are rarely more than five people at a time who even try.

Saturdays, however, thousands of little white balls are swept away. In their place, dozens of trucks and vans vie for space and attention with striped awnings rolled out over glass cases. The sign out front tastefully scrolled on a carved wooden plaque says, "Antique Mart." It lies. It describes rather pretentiously, in Connecticut vernacular, a flea market, plain and simple. It is unnerving, to say the least, to venture through an area hallmarked "antique" and be confronted with the very staples of my own immediate past. How, I wonder, when I feel as if I have barely lived, can I be viewing my own life as if it were already history?

When I see the jewel-colored aluminum tumblers stacked beside the sapphire blue pitcher, I can almost taste the lemonade my mother poured liberally on hot summer days and feel the cold metal against my tongue. I remember how I hated the feel of those drinking vessels against my mouth and how my fillings used to radiate with every swallow.

At the next booth I rediscover Barbie and silently berate myself for not having the foresight to retire my own doll and her regalia to the attic before the younger cousins arrived. I remember vividly the gold and white brocade evening gown with the genuine mink trim on the sleeves and the turquoise corduroy purse that didn't, to a nine-year-old's unsophisticated eye, seem to match at all. If I had them still, I could sell them here and take the cruise I have always dreamed of.

Across the aisle, I see a fox shawl dangling from a tarnished brass coat rack. It could well be the pair of foxes my great aunt Martha wore to Grandmother's house for Sunday dinners. The amber glass eyes in a fixed stare still have the power to intimidate me. The finely chiseled teeth end in points as sharp as cat's claws, and I can see myself at seven running down the hall with my cousin fast at my heels snapping the fox jaws with rabid growls.

And there is the music box, hiding dusty and neglected beside a Seth Thomas clock. It's just like the one my father gave my mother when he came home on his first leave from the army. When she lifted the lid the chimes played "Moonlight Serenade," but she hardly heard it. Her attention was riveted to the plain gold ring sparkling against the blue velvet background. There was no money for an engagement ring then. And during the war, there was little time for engagement.

Behind a battered blue van, I see our old kitchen dinette set. I remember standing on a footstool beside my mother and the feel of the smooth enameled table top beneath my hand as I put the raisins on gingerbread faces.

Rhinestones throw piercing shards of light that catch my eye. There's a large gaudy brooch—gold leaves entwined around three stems bearing glittering faux diamonds. I blush. This could be the one I gave my mother on her birthday. I walked the neighbors' dog a whole summer to save up $4. How her eyes brightened when she opened the box! That night my father took her out to a fancy restaurant. As she sat at her dressing table adding hairspray to her coiffure, I lay across the bed watching, waiting. And yes, she did. She pinned that brooch on her new black dress. She smiled at me in the mirror, and I was so proud. I thought my mother was the most glamorous woman in the world and if she wore it on such a special occasion, I knew she must really love it. I laugh out loud and ignore the people who turn with curious gazes to see what's funny. I can picture my mother removing the pin as soon as she got in the car. It was, after all, downright hideous.

Suddenly, the time warp shatters. Only two steps away skateboards painted fluorescent colors hang from ropes beside T-shirts stamped with gruesome creatures or brand names like "Adidas" and "Nike." As I leave, I find myself wondering what will be salvaged from my generation. What will my children find here twenty-five years from now? When they walk the aisles of tomorrow's "Antique Mart" touching and remembering, what will they remember about me?

113

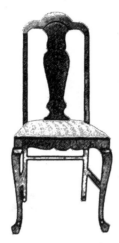

Fairy Tales

On the windowsill in my office, there is a collection of fairy tale characters in pliable, colorful plastic. You know, the kind you get at fast food places with your hamburgers and french fries. Mostly, I have the evil queens, witches, lions, and dragons. But I am still waiting for "Maleficent," the empress of evil in *Sleeping Beauty*. When I was five, my best friend Drew gave me the book *Sleeping Beauty* and I have treasured both the book and the story ever since.

My love for fairy tales cultivated my belief in happy endings. Princess Aurora, better known as Sleeping Beauty, lived happily ever after. In fairy tales there were always Fairy Godmothers waving magic wands to undo curses— turn rags into riches, pumpkins into chariots, and beasts and toads into princes. But for those of us trying to navigate life in the real world, the magic was much more complicated. And most of us had equal measure of Flora, Fauna, Merriweather and Maleficent flying about our nurseries bestowing gifts and curses.

I know now there are some basic truths to these fantastic fables. It occurs to me that the writers of fairy tales were artfully adept at defining and explaining the human psyche. Long before Oprah and Sally Jessy began hosting a platform for the psychologically impaired, the brothers Grimm had worked up quite a commentary on the human condition. Conjuring up wizards, talking fish, diminutive gold spinners, and insecure emperors, the authors make one point perfectly clear: a curse is a curse. There's no escaping it, and no amount of wishing will remove it. With a little insight and a lot of energy devoted to using your wits, your wiles, and your core set of principles, you can work around it. Sometimes, in the best of circumstances (and with a little magic) you can even make it work for you—like the miller's daughter who made off with the kingdom when she outsmarted Rumpelstiltskin.

I grew up with a love for fairy tales and fables, probably because my mother used familiar stories as well as some of her own imaginings to communicate some of life's tough lessons. I keep my colorful array of fairy tale antagonists on my windowsill to remind me that curses and spells can come in all sorts of unexpected packages.

"Even if you had a magic wand, he'd still be a toad," my mother once said, trying to ease the pain of my first heartbreak—Victor. "You can't turn him into a prince unless he was a prince in the first place. It would do you well to remember that." I laughed, despite the longing to ride in Victor's brand new yellow convertible and stare into the bluest eyes I had ever seen. As it turned out, she was right. No matter how nice I was to Victor, he was still a toad. These days, I hear he spends more time with his parole officer than his seven children.

"There's no such thing as a happy ending," my friend Jan says. But then, that's pretty much what fairy tales tell us. In fairy tales, wishes were rarely granted that weren't intended to plunge the wisher into misery or embarrassment—like King Midas who turned his daughter into gold, and the Fisherman and his Wife who were never satisfied. In fact, in all of these stories, the spells were not lifted until the cursed had proven themselves worthy by finding contentment in their circumstances, or in other words, found happiness within themselves.

After reading "The Emperor's New Clothes" aloud, my mother

patiently waited for my brother and me to stop giggling and pointing to the bare bony legs in the illustration. When her smile faded, we knew she was about to impart one of her moral or principle teachings. "The emperor's lesson is the hardest one to learn," she said. "And if you remember nothing else about this story, remember this. Things are what they are." She waited a moment and continued when the look of confusion on our faces intensified. She tried again. "Things just are what they are—not what you want them to be, not what they could be and not what someone else says they are—just what they are. And that will be okay as long as you believe in yourself enough to trust that what you see is what it really is."

I'm sure my brother and I must have looked at each other and rolled our eyes, just as we did when she insisted we add the "ly" to our adverbs and replace a "who" with a "whom." I'm also sure my mother sadly knew that this was another lesson we would both have to learn the hard way.

And like every parent that learned a tough lesson, I too have tried to spare my children the pain and humiliation that comes from learning the hard way. "What a dork," my son said of the emperor when he first heard the story ten years ago at age seven. "How could a king be so dumb? I would never do anything that stupid."

117

"I hope not, Bryan, but I sure did," I said. And then I told him about the time I didn't show up for the final cheerleading tryout because I was sure I wouldn't be chosen. And how I felt when I heard my name was called as a finalist, but the alternate got my position because I wasn't there.

"Bummer," he said.

"Really," I agreed.

"Hey, Mom," Bryan (now age seventeen) said in the car the other day on the way to our weekly breakfast out. "Remember that story about the emperor's clothes? Well, I think I get it."

His eyes stared straight ahead and his voice was flatly sad. "Do you want to talk about it?" I asked

"Not now," he said. "Maybe later." A minute later he added, "My girl-friend says there's no such thing as a happy ending. Do you believe that?"

"Well, I don't know if I believe in happily ever after," I said repressing the impulse to ask him what, if anything, had ended. "But my mother always told me every day is an opportunity to write a new chapter that can change the ending."

"Hm," he said. "That's pretty cool."

"Yeah," I said. "I guess it is."

Part Three

When the Dragons Wouldn't Die

It was hot. My hand was lost in his grip—his long fingers encircling mine. I could feel the sweat pooling between them. I could see the heat ripple in silky transparent waves from the street and feel the sun bounce off the sidewalk in white-hot sheets against my face. We walked on. My father's long stride was slow and patient, and his left arm swung loose at his side.

"Hey, Dick, how ya doin'?" Voices came tumbling from storefronts and sidewalk corners. I looked up to watch my father's face, and his smile fell across me like a cool and soothing shadow. Everyone knew him, this tall and handsome man who was my father, or so it seemed to me. Everyone knew his name, and knew him well enough to use it.

We walked on. He never dropped my hand. I never pulled mine from his grip. It was our day, our Sunday walk—the day each week when I was reminded of his strength, the day that he saw his reflection mirrored in my eyes. He was, at that moment, the most wonderful, most important man in the world, and he could save me from anything.

Last month, I drove over nine hundred miles to take that walk again. Childish imaginings and dreamed dragons had been replaced by real fears and pain that did not disappear at dawn. I needed my father to save me again.

This time we walked on gravel paths and didn't smile much. The sun danced and jumped between the trees almost in rhythm with the rusty sound of stones beneath our feet. Behind and all around us my dragons roared and thrashed—just out of sight, but there.

He listened and he shook his head. Anger creased the corners of his mouth and splashed cold light across his eyes. Someone had hurt his daughter, and my suffering made him angry. His shoulders sagged as anger turned to pain, my pain. He didn't understand divorce. He didn't understand leaving. He only knew his child was hurt, and someone was to blame.

He held it there, the weight of all my recent anguish, close to him, trying perhaps to keep it within himself and away from me, and feeling every ounce of it. I watched it weigh him down, pulling the strength from him. I watched his face and saw the truth—the truth neither one of us wanted to see. He could not save me this time.

When we said good-bye he held me close against his chest. "I wish there were something I could do," he said, "some way I could help you through this."

"I know, Dad," I answered, silently wishing the same. "I'll be fine. After all, I'm your daughter, and I'm a fighter."

As I backed away, he reached out and rested his hand on my shoulder. I looked up into his eyes. They were as bright as they had always been. The tears that gathered there gleamed in the sun and made them seem even brighter. "I love you, Jan," he said pushing his face to smile. "And I'm really proud of you."

I felt a sudden unfamiliar calmness. It spilled like liquid heat from my shoulder where his hand held on to me. "I love you too, Dad," I said smiling back.

Turning to leave, I felt the calmness thickening. It was taking shape and changing form. It was becoming strength. My father waved good-bye from the driveway. The sun, bouncing off the hood of the car, threw a blinding shaft of light. It looked for an instant like a gleaming sword tossed through the air.

I shook my head, and the illusion disappeared. It was time to go. I gathered all my dragons and took them home to fight.

Growing Pains

I couldn't find my son today. He was standing right in front of me, and I was looking right at him, but I couldn't find him. It was four o'clock the first day of cross-country practice, and there I was in the parking lot on time, squinting through the tinted glass windshield. In front of me stood a group of boys, tall and lean and barrel-chested, their faces sparsely dotted with telltale signs of adolescence. But these bodies had nothing to do with my son. My son is short and leggy, with shaggy blond hair and a toothy grin that usually sports evidence of cafeteria fare.

Suddenly the car door opens and one of those young men climbs into the back seat of my car. It's one of the taller ones, with broad sweat-glistened shoulders and thick muscular legs that end in shoes the size of boxes. As I turn to look at him he smiles and tosses his head slightly to the right so that his fawn-colored hair falls in a perfect arc curving away from his brow.

"Come on, Mom, I've got lots of homework to do." I can't respond. I am stunned that I have not seen this before—this man-child my son has become. When I start the car and turn back on to the road, I feel for an instant like I have awakened from a long sleep to find my life has gone on without me. I had closed my eyes holding hands with a blue-eyed, pixie-nosed boy who looked up at me full of questions and wonder, tears and confusion, laughter and joy. I have awakened, totally unprepared, to find myself eye-to-eye with a person who seems only slightly familiar.

It has been only a few short weeks since his thirteenth birthday. In fact, today when I walked into his room I noticed the thirteen balloons I hung from his ceiling light were still there. They hung limp and lifeless, entwined in blue ribbons and streamers. I laughed, remembering the first time he had awakened to balloons on his birthday and the following years when he tried to stay awake long enough to catch me hanging them. This year it was nearly 1 A.M. before I was sure he was sleeping deeply enough to pull it off.

At a stoplight I study him in the rearview mirror. His eyes catch mine and he smiles broadly. When had all those baby teeth disappeared? How many times had I forgotten to put the dollar under the pillow, seen the hurt in his face when he came downstairs for breakfast?

"No, honey, I'm sure the Tooth Fairy didn't forget you," I'd say. "Maybe it slipped under your bed. Go on up and look; I'll be right up to help you." If he knew I came to help look with the dollar concealed in my hand, he never let on. "Look at that!" I'd exclaim. "It fell into your shoe." Where is that gap-toothed smile now? When was it replaced by those two rows of even white squares?

"Can we stop for a drink, Mom? We did three miles today and I'm really thirsty." The voice from the back seat is strong and direct. There is no whining, no siren-like vowel extending my name into Maaaaaaaaaaom. When did that stop? And when did this boy who could not manage to walk three aisles at the mall gain the stamina to traverse three miles of Connecticut terrain?

I watch him as he strolls through the doors of the convenience store. Watching him, too, is a girl of about thirteen, standing beside her mother. She ducks her head as he walks by, then lifts her eyes to watch him as he opens the glass doors and picks out grape juice. Not yet, I say to her, with only myself to hear. You can't have him yet. It's too soon.

I feel a wave of sadness flow over me, resting on my shoulders like a heavy coat. It was too short, this time of nurturing. There were so many things we never did. So many things I never told him. Too many times I should have picked him up and held him close to me, felt his sweet baby's breath on my cheek. Too many times I should have said, "You're terrific."

The train set we planned to build a village for is still in its box at the bottom of his closet. The gasoline powered plane that requires adult supervision has never flown, and the quilt I always meant to make for his bed—the one with "Spirit of St. Louis" planes silhouetted in red and blue—was never even started.

As we pull up in front of the house, he bounds out before I've even put the car in park. "What do you know about parameciums, Mom? I've got a big test tomorrow and I need you to ask me questions after I study it, okay?" He disappears leaving only the sound of large footsteps echoing up the wooden stairs.

Reaching for the pantry door for tonight's supper ingredients, I see the blackboard, which was securely fastened there during the math crisis. From "one plus one" to "nine times nine," the black surface squeaked and flaked daily. White chalk powder became a part of our atmosphere. Today, it is blank except for a short message: "Jason call Ted."

"Okay, I'm ready," he shouts, his voice accented by the thump of his descent. Into the kitchen he waltzes, his books in one hand, the string of deflated balloons tumbling behind him. The faint thumping of deflated rubber bouncing against itself trails him like a herd of miniature elephants. "I think it's time to throw these away, don't you?" he asks smiling.

"I guess you're right,'" I say, taking the tangled mass from his hand. Then I wrap my arms around his shoulders and hold him tightly against me. "You're terrific," I say, my eyes burning, close to tears.

He hugs me back, despite his apparent awkwardness. I am glad his head still tucks beneath my chin. "You're terrific too, Mom," he says, not pulling away, as if he knows I'm the one who has to let go first.

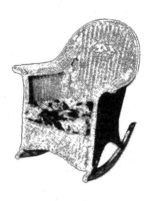

Balancing Lessons

When I was six years old, my cousin Jamie was the only person I knew close to my age that didn't have a mother. I had only a faint memory of her. She was sitting on the sand beside the lake smiling calmly, while my cousin, her son, waved back at her from a raft that bobbed gently in the middle of the water. I remember thinking how brave he was, daring to cross a lake that looked to me black and bottomless—and how confident his mother seemed, as if she knew for sure that he was safe.

After his mother died, Jamie spent more time with my family and me than he probably cared to. Three nights a week and on Sundays he was shuffled between our grandmother and his two aunts, one of whom was my mother. All of his cousins were female, and although he tolerated us well, he couldn't help but roll his eyes when we dragged out our paper dolls and "Millie the Model" comic books.

One Sunday after church, I followed Jamie out into the street where he had planned to meet his best friend, Jeff. It was a typical Sunday afternoon at my grandmother's. There wasn't a lot of time between church and Sunday dinner, and we were expected to stay quiet, out of the way, and impeccably dressed.

I stood on the bottom step of my grandmother's house watching him kick rocks into the sewer grate—listening to the hollow echo of their bounce as they tumbled into darkness below the street. He hadn't said anything all day—hadn't teased me or called me a name. I wondered if he was thinking about his mother. But when he finally talked, it wasn't about his mother, it was about Betsy. His mother had bought him a bike shortly before she became ill, and he had named it Betsy. From that day on, it stood less than three feet from him whenever he was outside. He would lean it gently against a telephone pole or the side of the house, but never on the ground. Betsy had no kick stand, because he said they sometimes came loose and got in the way when you were racing. But it had a hand brake and a battery powered horn that sounded like my grandfather's old pink pick-up truck.

I never knew anyone that named a bicycle, but then again, I didn't know anyone with a bike as special as Betsy. She was sleek and fire-engine red, and everyone knew she was the fastest bike in the neighborhood.

"When are you getting a bike?" he asked, swinging his leg over Betsy's seat, stopping to roll up the right leg of his good Sunday pants.

"I don't know," I answered. "I can't ride a bike. My dad wants to get me one with training wheels."

"That's baby stuff," he sneered while riding Betsy in tight circles in the middle of the street. "You don't need sissy training wheels. Besides, how will you ever learn to balance if you're leaning on those stupid wheels all the time?"

I kind of knew what he meant. My best friend, Donna, had gotten a bike for her birthday three months before, and she still had the training wheels on. I would see her ride by on the sidewalk in front of my house, with her bike leaning one way and her body leaning the other, so together, they almost formed an arrow.

"Come on," he said, jumping off without stopping and leading Betsy to the sidewalk. "I'll show you. It's easy." He stood in front of me and patted Betsy's seat. He was still wearing the bow tie he had on in church, and I still had on my dark plaid dress. All the grown-ups were in my grandmother's

128

house, and their cars lined the street forming a tunnel with the sidewalk and overhanging trees.

I had been on Betsy many times, but never on the seat. Jamie would hoist me up on the thick red bar between the seat and handle bars and sail me down the hill between my grandmother's house and mine. Sometimes he'd take me down Nickels Hill to the hardware store for a new skate key, or to the tavern parking lot behind Donna's house where we searched for lost change in the gravel. But never had I ever seen anyone but Jamie on Betsy's seat.

With his help, I stepped on the pedal and threw my leg over. "But my feet don't touch the ground," I protested, starting to feel nervous.

"You don't need the ground, dummy," he laughed. "You only need the pedals. If you feel yourself leaning, then lean back the other way, but not too far. It's easy!" We began to move, Betsy, Jamie and I. He held the back of Betsy's seat with his right hand and one of the handlebars with the left. Soon he was running, Betsy's pedals were flying and I was riding. "Don't let go," I pleaded. "I don't know how to stop."

"Don't worry," he shouted. "I've got you." We circled the entire block and I held my breath every time Betsy's wheels thudded over cracks in the sidewalk. Before I knew it, we were back in front of the garage where we started. Betsy slowed and the weight of us leaned against Jamie's side. His face was flushed and his bow tie was slightly askew. "See, what'd I tell ya? You don't need sissy training wheels. You've got balance."

"No, I don't," I said struggling to get off Betsy and hold my dress down at the same time. "You were holding me up."

"No, I wasn't," he answered, his mouth lifting to a smile I had not seen on him all day. "I let go of you in front of the Stones' house and you rode all the way here by yourself."

"You lied," I railed at him. "You said you would hold me up."

"Did not," he answered. "I said I've got you. How else do you think you're gonna learn to ride a stupid bike, anyway?"

He pulled Betsy away from my grasp, and I saw the smile fade from his face. "I don't lie," he said, pushing Betsy toward the house. "I said I had you, and I did. I wouldn't have let you fall." Jamie was three years older than I was but not much bigger. Even so, at that moment, he seemed bigger and stronger to me then anybody else I knew, except my father. The next Sunday, when he let me get back on Betsy again, I never doubted for a minute that I was safe.

A few months later I got my own bicycle—without training wheels. Jamie and I would ride together once in a while when his friends weren't around or when the families got together on Sundays. That summer, he'd come to our house every Thursday night for dinner. We'd sit on the front porch, and he'd teach me how to whistle, or tell me a gory ghost story I could, in turn, use to horrify my friends. In the winter, he taught me how to ice skate backwards and how to make paper jets that flew all the way across the living room.

The following summer, we moved away, and leaving Jamie was harder than leaving my best friend Donna. He still hadn't taught me to throw a football with a spiral, because my hands were not yet big enough. And he had promised to teach me to dive off the diving board at Black Rock Lake.

Two decades later, we were living no more than ten miles apart once again—but now we were both single parents, struggling to make sense of where we'd been and where we needed to go. And like old friends, we came together as if a thousand miles and twenty years had never separated us. We sat around my kitchen table pouring tea from our grandmother's teapot, trying to cheer each other up by talking about the old neighborhood and the day he taught me to ride Betsy. "You were a pretty fast learner for a girl," he teased. "That's what I liked about you."

"Hey, you were a pretty good teacher," I said, squeezing his shoulder as I passed by him on route to the stove.

He may have been thinking about my daring attempt to take corners on my bike without touching the handlebars, because I had seen him and Betsy do it. Or maybe he was remembering the time I risked life and limb jumping over the barrel on Blake's pond after watching him do it at hockey practice.

I stopped thinking about tomorrow and wondering how I would get through the day. Instead, I was remembering the feel of the hot summer wind against my face and the strength I felt pushing Betsy's pedals. And then, for a minute, I was back on my own midnight blue English racer, careening corners five feet ahead of the neighborhood bully, Gene Nepolotano, racing toward the street sign we had designated as the finish line. Jamie was there, waving me on. As I slowed to a stop, I heard him say. "Hey, that's my cousin. She's only seven and she beat you!"

"You know, Jamie," I said, pouring more tea into his cup. "I've learned a lot from you."

"Why?" he asked, averting his eyes and blushing slightly. "Because I wouldn't let you let you use those sissy training wheels?"

"Exactly," I said, and left it at that.

Folding Time

On my desk, there is a picture of an eight-year-old boy. His face is open in wonder, in delight of the moment and anticipation of the future. There are two teeth missing in front, so his smile is hesitant, but only from the outside. His big blue eyes are arched high as if asking, "What's next?" His smile is so unself-conscious that his cheekbones are raised against his bottom lids, and one wonders if he could laugh and see at the same time.

His back is straight and his neck stretches long and proudly. Coarse straight hair is tossed in an angle across a high forehead. This is a child with a thousand questions to ask, hundreds of puddles yet to jump, two dogs still to name and cry over, pages of math homework to hand in, and countless heartaches yet to survive. This is my son. Beside him, on the same desk, is a tall handsome young man in a white dinner jacket and black bow tie. On his arm is a pretty blonde in pink and white satin. This is the same son. And the time it took for him to jump from one picture to the next seems no longer than the time it takes me now to look from one to the other.

I keep the little one on my desk to remind me. He is still my child. The eyes that stare from the frame in wonder are the same eyes that sparkle with masked embarrassment from the junior prom picture. They have the same capacity for tears, just as they have the same wide potential for delight. They are narrowed some now by restrictions on "coolness."

When my son stretches both his limits and mine by arguing a little too loudly, by defying a little too long, I look at this wide-eyed urchin grinning atop my desk and try to remember him. I look into his eyes, and I see the determination that kept him on the street in front of our house for five hours with his new bicycle until he could finally sail away from the curb unaided. I see the compassion he showed his baseball teammates when they struck out. There's the kindness he showed Miss Margaret next door on her ninetieth birthday when he asked me if we could bake her a cake. I see the generosity that compelled him to spend forty dollars of his hard-earned money on a basketball his brother would love. In this child there is an unbridled curiosity about the nature of people combined with openness and trust.

Beside him, in formal attire, his taller version appears much changed. Perhaps the beaming blonde beside him will give his heart a yank and twist that may cloud even more the eyes that once believed in Superman and Santa Claus. Or perhaps the one before her is the reason his smile only reaches half as high on one side. Maybe it was failing to make the basketball team that lowered the arch in his eyebrow, or missing the varsity ski team by three points that pushed his shoulders a little forward.

134

When I look at him in this picture, resplendent in James Bond garb, I can hear the cockiness in his voice as he tells me, "Don't worry, Mom, I'll pull the grades up by June." The same child who was once so eager to please me that he brought me tea in bed every Saturday before turning on his cartoons now often finds it difficult to say "good morning" when he passes me in the hallway.

Sitting here, glancing back and forth between past and present, I feel somewhat suspended between times. And then, outside the window, I hear the lawnmower roar to life. I pull the curtains aside to see my son, a T-shirt in place of the dinner jacket and the toothless smile pulled into a broad grin full of wide, straight teeth. He waves widely and I wave back. Then he turns—his strong lean back pushed into a determined effort as he sets his course along a straight line down the yard.

I look again at the boys in the two photographs, and I miss them both. It feels as if they were people I knew once. But outside this window is my son. So I think I'll get up and make him some iced tea.

Change of Hearts

It's raining in Bridgeport when the ferry finally docks. My son is standing near the gate, a suitcase at his feet, watching as the crewmen toss ropes and secure hinges. They've done it a thousand times, these men, but today it seems like a terrible ritual. I know my son's eyes are glistening and his throat aches when he tries to swallow. It's a simple thing; he's going back to school. He's getting on this ferry to meet a friend who will drive him nine hundred miles away, and he's saying good-bye.

Just in front of him, less than a breath away, is his girlfriend. This young beauty is staring into his saddened eyes and promising him the love and comfort he needs to get on that ferry.

I'm sitting in the car one hundred feet away, because this moment no longer belongs to me. When I look at him, I still see a frightened little boy on the first day of kindergarten, clinging to a Superman lunch box and fighting back tears with brave predictions like, "They'll have toys there, won't they Mommy? You'll come back and pick me up if I don't like it here, won't you Mommy?" In my heart I still feel the grip of his fear when he comes running back to the car and pleads, "Please don't make me go in there." Back then I was the one who hugged him tightly and promised to be there for him. When his outstretched arms grasped for reassurance, my arms were the ones that enfolded him. Today, I watch a strange hand reach up and touch his cheek. Someone else's words bring life back into his eyes—someone who looks into his face and sees a man where my little boy once stood. I watch his shoulders shake and I know he's laughing. Whatever she said to him has worked, and he feels strong again.

People board the ferry like an exodus, milling past the unmoving couple. Jason turns and looks toward the car and forces a smile. I get out of the car and wave, resisting the impulse to shout, "You better go before the ferry leaves you." We said our good-byes a few minutes earlier—good-byes full of reminders like, "Try to find time to send your grandfather a note; he misses you." and "Please don't let that fraternity interfere with your schoolwork." He hugged me tightly, because he knew I needed it. Now my reminders are out of place. He'll board the ferry on time because it's important to him.

He bends to pick up his suitcase and she lets go of him for an instant. Even from this distance I know her good-bye is different from mine. She's telling him that she'll write every day. She's on her tiptoes now, her arms thrown frantically around his neck, wishing with every millisecond that passes that she had thousands more. He holds her face in one hand and kisses her lightly good-bye before he pulls away. He turns to me one more time and waves, without a smile this time.

As she walks toward me I can see this will not be an easy ride home for her. When she pulls the car door shut, I reach out and pat her on the shoulder. I want to say anything I can that will make her ache stop, but I know it's useless. I want to say that he'll be home again in three weeks, and that's not such a long time. I want to tell her how I felt the first September he went off to school, and how I sat on his bed and held his Mr. Spock doll and cried. But I don't say anything because I realize that I have just said a special good-bye of my own. Tonight when Jason gets back to his dorm, it won't be memories of his room and his home that sadden him. When he gets lonely or frightened, it won't be my phone that rings.

Driving away, I stop the car and turn to look behind me. Jason stops at the same time and turns to look for us. I knew he would. He always has. The young girl beside me leans out the window and waves broadly. Even through tears her smile is warm and safe, and I know Jason's long journey back to school will be easier because of it.

The next night, when I answer the phone I'm glad to hear his voice is more cheerful than the last time I heard it. "I just wanted to tell you I made it okay," he says.

"I miss you already," I say, just realizing it myself.

"I miss you too," he answers out of kindness. "And Mom," he hesitates. "Thanks."

"For what?" I ask.

"Oh, you know," he says, almost shyly. "For taking us to the ferry."

I know what he really means is, "Thanks for not holding on too tightly. Thanks for letting me be grown up, at least in front of my girlfriend. And thanks for letting me think I'm in love without telling me I'm too young to know what it's all about."

"No problem," I say. But it is. It really is.

137

Out of My League

It's a Saturday morning in spring. For a brief moment I think I hear my son stirring, scavenging through piles of unwashed clothes that are billowing out his closet doors. In a dream I must have heard him yell, "Mom, I can't find my catcher's mitt. I bet Jason has it. I'm gonna kill him!"

From the other end of the hallway, I imagine I hear the familiar response. "Mom, tell Bryan I don't have his stupid mitt, but he has my bat and I want it back." When I am fully awake, I realize this is a scene from my past. A scene I relived hundreds of times throughout the ten years that I was a Little League mother.

In other houses in my neighborhood this incident is really happening but with different names, because . . . baseball season has begun. All over town mothers are groping the insides of dryers looking for the missing baseball sock. Dads are glancing at their watches and revving motors in driveways. Kids are grabbing Pop-Tarts out of toasters and diving under beds and behind doors looking for cleats. Everywhere household chatter chimes with, "Mom, where did you put my hat?" and "Mom, my shoelace is busted, can you find me a new one?"

My house is silent. The baseball equipment lies in a dusty heap in the back of the garage. Once in a while the dog picks up the ball and drops it again. There's no reason to run with it, because there's no one to chase her for it.

I suppose I should be glad that I don't have a pair of white baseball pants soaking in a bleach-filled kitchen sink or a dust-coated batter's glove tossed on my dining room table. I guess I should delight in planning a selfish Saturday of shopping or reading, knowing I don't have to rush to the ball field and spend the morning swatting mosquitoes and dodging foul balls.

This year I won't be sitting with clenched teeth and crossed fingers when my son comes up to bat with two outs and the bases loaded. I won't be there to nod in frowning agreement as the mothers complain about the umpire. And when little Johnny misses the high fly to left field, I can't listen sympathetically as his mother tells us that his eyes are extremely sensitive to sunlight.

Today I won't be there to hear the groans of despair with every slide to home or to shake my head and wonder out loud why the town insists on buying white pants for the uniforms.

I have an entire Saturday stretched before me with a multitude of choices, but nothing seems to motivate me. I am stuck in the past remembering my days in the league. I can still see the look of shocked delight on Jason's face when he peered into his glove and realized he'd caught the line drive to second. There's a clear picture of Bryan bounding across home plate on a triumphant home run after a sad series of strikeouts. On the good days we all high-fived in the car on the way home, because it was only okay for me to show my pride in private. On bad days we walked in silence to the car and I resisted powerful urges to hug them and say I knew things would get better. On those days we'd go to the drive-in for hot dogs and milk shakes. There, the other team members would congregate and tell each other they lost the game on bad calls.

At home I did hug them and tried all the dumb cliches for which mothers are notorious. With each subsequent ride to the ballpark, they fought discouragement with valor and jokes, while I tossed silent prayers skyward. With each hit that almost was and each grounder that passed between their legs uncaught, my heart would leap and fall.

As the seasons unfolded there were fewer and fewer misses. There were more daring moves, more attempts to throw home from center field, more stolen bases. My boys weren't necessarily the MVPs, but they managed to keep up. Each year, as the competition grew fiercer, the will to win became more powerful and the bonds between team members grew stronger. Rarely did a player roll his eyes in disgust when the catcher missed a pop fly or a batter failed to swing at a perfect pitch. They were growing up.

I watched as these characteristics transcended the ball field and showed up at home. I heard Jason coaching his younger brother on how to survive his freshman year of high school, and overheard Bryan encouraging his older brother to ask the "hot new sophomore" to the senior prom. On more than one occasion they could be heard in unison pleading, "Go for it, Mom! You can do it," as I fearfully approached the intermediate ski slope.

Maybe they would have been the same boys if they had stayed home on Saturdays gluing model cars or arranging stamp collections; then again, maybe not.

My mournful musings are interrupted by a deep masculine voice from outside my bedroom door. "Mom, are you up?" Jason calls. "I get off work at three. You want to play some golf?"

"I don't know . . ." I hesitate, still thickly involved in self-pity.

"Come on, don't be a wimp," he says, poking his smiling face through the door. "I think I can help you with that slice. You know," he adds with a coaxing tone I must have tried on him hundreds of times through the years, "you won't get good at it if you don't practice."

Somewhere in the distance I think I hear someone yell, "Batter up!"

Marissa's Magic

My friend Marissa has beautiful hair. It's the color of wheat in the late afternoon sun, shot with hot streaks of fire yellow. When she tosses her head, her hair catches the light—any light—and brilliant shards of silver dance through it. Every so often, she will arch her back slightly, place both hands behind her head and fan her hair out over her hands ever so slowly, letting the ribbons of soft gold glide through her fingers and fall in shimmering waves against her shoulders and waist. There is much delight in her gestures, and her movements are fluid and deliberate. You can't help but watch her.

Marissa is seven years old, and I didn't know she had beautiful hair until she told me.

The first time I saw her she was staring hollow-eyed from a photograph. The light in the picture was harsh, and Marissa's small face was set in a rigid pose, as if she had held a smile too long. She seemed thin and pale, her skin almost blue beneath her large gray eyes. When I first met her, she looked much the same. She was sitting at the kitchen table flipping through a small picture book. She paid little attention to me, looking up to say a polite hello. Her eyes caught mine for an instant, and they seemed at once blue and green, and then gray again. She was thin and frail with bones that seemed determined to show in jagged forms beneath her pale skin.

All through dinner, Marissa eyed me suspiciously. I was a new friend to this family, and judging from her unwavering stare, I would be carefully scrutinized before her approval would be issued.

As the last dish was cleared and we all returned to our seats for coffee, I found Marissa standing beside my chair. She stood with one hand resting on the table, and as I slipped past her I felt much like a defendant about to take the stand at my own trial. But Marissa surprised me. She slid onto my chair beside me, urging me with a gentle nudge to give her room. Then looking up at me through peacock lashes she said, "I have beautiful hair, you know. My dad says I could be in a shampoo commercial." For an instant, I could not respond. Because I had not, in fact, noticed that Marissa's hair was particularly beautiful. Instead, I was rather struck by the apparent unhealthiness of her entire being. I didn't know the specifics of Marissa's illness. I knew only that she suffered from asthma and that her diet was closely monitored.

Before I could reply, she lifted my hand from my lap and placed in on her head. "You can feel it if you want," she said, tilting her head back. "It's very soft."

She was right. Her hair was not only soft, but it felt thick and smooth beneath my hand. "Your daddy's right," I said. "You do have beautiful hair. I wish I had hair like that."

"Don't be silly," she said matter-of-factly. "You can't just wish it. You have to believe it."

With that, Marissa rose from my seat and executed an effortless pirouette across the dining room floor. Her hair rose from her shoulders in a perfect swirl like a fountain in the moonlight, and she seemed suddenly a healthy, vibrant child. "I see," I said, eager to hear more about this young one's philosophy. "Is that what you do?"

"Oh, yes," she said. "I do that with everything. I mean—if it's okay with God. You know, like, I never believe bad things." As she spoke, I had to remind myself that I was listening to a seven-year-old. She moved close to me, and then, placing both hands on my shoulders, leaned forward as if she were about to share a very private secret. "You know," she said, her eyes darting from side to side, making sure her secret would be shared with only me, "if you believe bad things, you will feel bad. And if you feel bad, you can't make good things happen."

I was stunned. It was such a simple truth, but at the same time, such a powerful choice for a child to make—for anyone to make. I studied her carefully as she danced away from me, spinning the skirt of her dress into a flat circle around her waist. "I'm going to be a very famous dancer someday," she said as she twirled. "Do you believe that?"

"Yes," I answered. "I believe that." And I do.

145

Mattie's Quilt Goes Home

Every few minutes a large, overstuffed, and carelessly taped box hoisted onto broad shoulders cruises through the kitchen and out the back door. I'm standing at the stove wondering if the Bavarian custard will ever thicken or if I misread the recipe. I wonder too if I'm just thinking of things to fret about so I don't have to acknowledge that 30 percent of my household is exiting out the back door.

I notice that the box coming around the corner is bulging open, and a large shaft of bright yellow is pushing its way out. "Jason," I say. "You're not taking the quilt are you?"

Jason puts the box down in the middle of the floor and collapses onto a chair. He pulls off his baseball hat and a tumbling mass of bangs falls into his eyes. I refuse to notice the thick stubble darkening his chin, because I know I can't be old enough to have a child that can grow a beard.

Now the box has completely opened and the startlingly yellow "Lone Star of Texas" quilt has escaped and is draped down the side of the box onto the floor. I bend to pick it up—quickly—as if it's a treasured pet at risk of injury on the tile floor. Until that moment, I'm sure I did not actually believe my son was leaving.

Jason smiles and I know he's remembering the day we found the quilt. It was a summer of adventure, the first time just the three of us ventured across the states to visit my parents. "Let's take some back roads," Jason said twelve hours into the trip with the atlas spread across his lap. "Come on, Mom, we learned how to read maps in geography. I can do this. This interstate is boring."

I remember feeling skeptical. I doubted if his sixth grade teacher had spent much time navigating the mountains of East Tennessee, or that Jason, in his infinite eleven-year-old wisdom, realized that a flat blue line on paper could very well be a thirty-eight-degree climb up a Smoky Mountain range.

"Highway 58," he said excitedly. "Take that." And we did. The road narrowed immediately and tossed us into a deep "S" curve that burrowed into a hillside. To the right of us, the embankment seemed to meet the road at a 90-degree angle only inches beyond the car door. On the other side, the earth fell away sharply showing us only lanky treetops at eye level.

That's when we saw it. Just a mile past Junior's Texaco station. A stream of color burst across the landscape like a giant kite tail. "Stop!" Jason yelled pointing at the color. "Look, Mom, quilts. Let's stop."

Teetering on the edge of a steep embankment was a front porch balancing precariously on three stacks of concrete blocks. Strung across the porch end to end was a row of mammoth squares pieced in discernible patterns of vibrant colors. A cardboard sign nailed to a post slightly off center limped in the breeze. "Mattie's handmade quilts 4 sale," was scrawled beneath the nail in black—the same black that gleamed on the freshly painted mailbox at the bottom of the gravel drive.

"Come on Mom, you've wanted a quilt forever. You've got to stop." We pulled into the driveway, and as we approached, I became more and more apprehensive. These were not like the quilts I had envied in *Better Homes and Gardens* or even the ones I had seen in craft stores in Vermont. Those had muted hues of pastel greens, soft roses and cloudy blues. Mattie's quilts were vibrant colors like the colors of the grass that grew in large clumps at the base of her porch and the red geraniums that bent forward from all manner and col-

148

ors of plastic pots lining the porch steps. One quilt in the middle was so yellow the dandelions seemed pale in comparison.

By the time I had the emergency brake engaged, Jason was already out of the car waving to an older woman I guessed must be Mattie. In the back seat, Bryan, who did not share his brother's enthusiasm for spontaneous diversions, rolled his eyes and flipped on his computer game.

When I caught up with Jason he was of course standing in front of the dandelion quilt. "Check it out, Mom. This one is really cool!" In the center of what appeared to be an acre of caution-light yellow was a massive five-pointed star intricately pieced together with two-inch long diamonds of various prints and colors. The quilting stitches followed the star pattern then channeled into straight lines about an inch apart on the yellow background. Mattie was smiling at Jason as she lifted her gnarled hand toward the quilt. "The stitches ain't as straight as I used to make 'um," she said shaking her head. "But then again, I can't see as good as I used to so it don't bother me much." She brushed the quilt with her hand as if she were smoothing out a wrinkle.

"This one here took up the last of my green calico," she added, pointing to the center where a circle of lime green diamonds marked the beginning of the starburst of color. "When my Martha was in home economics class, we bought this here to make aprons for her project." She laughed and shook her head. "Martha must have thought she was making aprons for a herd of elephants, cause we had so much left over, I've used it on nearly every quilt I've made since." Jason and I laughed with her, and at that moment, we both knew that quilt would be going back to Connecticut with us. Suddenly the yellow seemed more invitingly warm than garishly bright.

For the past ten years, Mattie's yellow-star quilt has decorated Jason's room in various capacities—a bed spread, a wall hanging and once even a tent for his younger brother. From the time it arrived, there was a sort of transformation. Never again did I have to tell him to make his bed or remind him to deposit his wet towels in the laundry basket, not on the bed. My grandfather's desk was retrieved from the basement, polished, and placed at the foot of his

149

bed. Jason's father's trophies lined a shelf Jason had found himself at a tag sale. From Mattie's quilt bloomed Jason's sanctuary.

Now the sanctuary would be somewhere else. I know that as I clutch the quilt and stare into my son's eyes that are red rimmed and glistening. I remember now the conversations about the great apartment he's found back in the state where he was born, about his commitment to finish school in two years as a Tennessee resident. I had blocked it all out, until now. "Don't cry, Mom," he says. I hold the quilt out and open my arms to hug him. We both know the quilt is going back to Tennessee with him where it belongs.

No Small Measure

When my children were young, they would routinely ask to be measured. I would stand them against the inside of the pantry door in my kitchen. "Heels flat on the floor," I'd say. "Stand up straight." Then, I'd place a sturdy piece of cardboard on each head and mark each one's initials, height, and date with a pencil.

Their bodies seemed to stop growing about the same time we moved into a house with no pantry and no discreetly hidden location in which to chart their growth. Naively, I believed I could stop measuring progress. But once we stopped documenting inches, they began other competitive comparisons, measuring themselves against each other, and then finally, me against the world of "real mothers."

"Jason had a car when he was seventeen," Bryan laments.

"Jason had a job when he was seventeen," I retort.

"I couldn't do anything when I was seventeen. You let Bryan get away with murder," Jason reminisces with a moan.

"It's true, Mom." Bryan says, allying with his brother. "You were tougher on him."

"For instance . . ." I say, because I'm interested in knowing what I had done that was bad enough to cause Bryan to sympathize, rather than argue, with his brother.

"Don't you remember the time you wouldn't let him go up to Rich's house just because it was after 8:30? He was sixteen."

"No, I remember when I wouldn't let him leave the house after 10:30, and he was only fifteen."

"Whatever," Bryan says, undeterred. "You yelled at him a lot."

"Did I?" I ask, not because I don't believe him but because I do, and am surprised that Bryan noticed. "Didn't I yell at you?"

"Not as much." He's probably right. I think with the second son there's a certain resignation that takes over. Knowing how the story turns out removes a lot of the drama and anxiety, so I picked fewer battles the second time around. I'm not sure they fully grasp the concept, so I try an analogy they can relate to. "Were you as scared the second time you saw *Friday the 13th*?"

"Okay, I get it," Bryan concedes. But still I find this conversation unsettling.

I thought I had finally gotten to the point where I could relax, take a deep breath and say to myself, "Good, the hard part's over now. They're gown up and have not been cataloged "repeat offenders" by the juvenile justice department. But I can't, because now that I've finished the job I'm being evaluated, and I don't seem to measure up.

These ad-lib criticisms just pop out during ordinary moments, and I am always surprised both by the impromptu nature of the complaint and by its significance in their lives. If both sons happen to be in the same room at the same time, it begins to sound like an auction of accusations, each one attempting to out suffer the other.

Jason, finding the sympathetic atmosphere inviting, interjects his own memories of torture. "Remember the time you went out to eat and forgot to pick me up from ski practice? I had to walk all the way home with all my equipment." That I remember, and the image of Jason dodging blinding headlights with skis balanced on his shoulder still makes me wince.

"You weren't very friendly to my friends," Bryan chimes in, attempting to capitalize on the moment. "They all thought you didn't like them." Now I've had about enough. All of his friends have grown up and moved away to college, and I can do little if anything about endearing them to me. I could spend a lot of time wishing I had known what my children needed from me when they needed it. The fact is, I didn't get it right all of the time.

I suppose for me guilt is the emotion that lies closest to the surface and is most easily evoked. Lately, however, I've developed an exercise that allows me to control it. I no longer attempt to contradict my sons' memories. Whether they really happened or not, their memories have become their history. At the same time, I don't want to wallow in a past we can't change. Instead, when they begin to recite the litany of my sins, real or imagined, I ask them to come up with at least one thing I did during the same time period that was particularly nice. Sometimes, I have to assist them. "Come on," I say, trying not to plead. "I couldn't have been that bad. After all, you turned out pretty well."

"Okay, I've got one," Bryan volunteers after an uncomfortable pause. "Remember the time some kid handcuffed Jason and I together and ran away with the key? You had to get out of the shower to pick the lock with your nail file."

I don't remember that at all. And it's not exactly what I had in mind, because I don't think it fits the "exceptional" criteria. When I shrug acceptance, Bryan seems to notice my disappointment.

"You're okay, Mom," he says and kisses my cheek. "Sometimes you're even cool." I'm not sure where that ranks me on his standard of measurement, but I think I passed. And for now, that's good enough.

The Father
I Remember

At sixty-five my father says he has a lot of regrets. Mostly I hear about them when he's at my house and has just witnessed a scene involving my oldest child and his over-protective, over-critical, unrelenting mother. At times like this, my father appears to be the patron saint of patience and understanding. For some reason, I do not remember this side of him.

"You're too hard on him," my father says as my son retreats muttering inaudible yet unmistakably slanderous comments under his breath. "You've got to take more time to listen to him—try to understand how he feels. I wish I had spent more time talking to you kids when you were younger."

My hackles are up. I want to retaliate in kind with litanies of his false accusations and criticisms of the past. I want to remind him of his slightly less-than-perfect parental participation, but I don't. I am stilled by the look of sadness that slides across his face. He's remembering years of dinner meetings and business trips, the midget-league ball games he missed and the picnics that were postponed until after the eighteenth hole.

I take myself back to the time he's replaying, and I see him as a blur—a dark gray suit with a red tie. He's in the kitchen with an arm around my mother and he's laughing—and then he's gone. As the door closes behind him the notes from the Frank Sinatra tune he was singing are shut off, and the house is silent.

We didn't talk much, true. The days spun quickly on an axis of hellos and good-byes. There were more hasty commands than profound discussions and more pecked cheeks than hugs. But there were, on occasion, family soft-ball games and midnight breakfasts with cheese omelets and Irish jokes. There were times when my father laughed so hard he cried, and there were times when he simply cried.

We are jolted to the present by the sound of Huey Lewis pouring out of the speakers of Jason's stereo. My father smiles and shakes his head. His new-found understanding stops short of rock music.

I reach out and touch his shoulder. "I'm doing the best I can, Dad," I say.

He smiles and pats my hand. He's looking out the window watching my youngest son shooting baskets alone in the back yard. "I think I'll go shoot some hoops," he says walking past me and out the door.

For a while I stand and watch the two of them. The sound of their laugh-ter glides across the lawn on the late afternoon breeze. "Can you teach me that shot, Pop?" Bryan pleads with unmasked admiration. My father laughs again.

Standing alone in my kitchen, I am laughing too. I am remembering the night before my first dance when my father taught me how to fox trot. "Just relax and let me lead," he said. "And don't look at your feet." I remem-ber the feel of his massive hand pressing against my back and the smell of his after-shave floating beside us as we moved. The plush green carpet seemed to grow into serpentine strands that wrapped around my ankles and thwarted every attempt I made to follow him. "You go stand over there," he said, "and watch your mother."

She stepped into his arms and looked back at me smiling. They paused a second and then swept into motion. He towered over her by nearly a foot, but they seemed a single unit—gliding in perfect rhythm around the room, turning at every corner and never taking their eyes from each other. I learned how to dance that night—enough to carry me through four years of homecoming dances and junior/senior proms. But I never danced like they did.

"Great shot, Pop." Bryan's voice erases the scene. Words follow, first my father's then Bryan's, but they are too far away to be distinct. I hear a door close and I know Jason has joined them. "Hey Pop, I need some help with my hook shot."

My father comes in and stands beside me. He wipes his face with his monogrammed handkerchief and wraps his long strong arm around my shoulders.

"Those guys are too much for me," he says with a laugh. Then his face becomes serious and he squeezes me a little tighter. "They're great kids, Jan. You're doing a terrific job."

"Thanks Dad," I say. "I had a great teacher."

He smiles, and I know in that instant that it's true. And now maybe we'll both spend less time thinking about regrets and a little more time cherishing the laughter. "Thanks," he says in return. "I did the best I could."

"I know Dad," I say, hugging him back. "I know."

In just a few days he'll be gone again, and the house will seem half-empty for a long time. I picture my sons after my father has gone back to Tennessee. Night after night Bryan will bounce the ball in the hard grassless circle that has become his kingdom, and Jason will stand in the kitchen with his arms crossed testing my limited knowledge of politics while I cook. At dinner we'll talk about my father, just as we do after each of his visits.

"I miss Pop," Bryan will say. "It's boring around here without him."

"It must have been great having him for a Dad," Jason will say again. "He's so interesting to talk to."

I could tell them this is not the man I grew up with. But of course it is. It's just a calmer, more contemplative version. I could tell them about the conversations that were often one-sided and occasionally loud. But I'd have to tell them about the way I slammed my bedroom door—or the time I walked out in the middle of dinner and didn't come back until 3:00 A.M. But I won't. Instead, I'll let them keep the vision they have of both of us now. It pleases us all.

"Yes," I'll say. "He is pretty cool. And did I ever tell you about the time he taught me to dance?"

The Harry Chronicles

Last night I sat at the dinner table with my son and his two friends. If it weren't for an occasional apology offered for inappropriate language, I would have thought they were completely unaware of my presence. I listened in amusement as they reenacted scenes from a movie they had watched together the week before. I smiled when Donald (affectionately known as Deek) strummed a hard-rock tune on an imaginary guitar; listened sympathetically when J.O.N. (pronounced spelled out to distinguish him from John) announced he wouldn't be running track in college because of his knee injury.

Eventually, they got around to the age-old question that has plagued young men for generations: "Why is it that the best looking girls are never the ones that talk to us?" That was a question I probably could have answered, some enlightenment I probably could have shared, not necessarily because of my age and experience, but because of my gender. What better way to understand females than to ask one?

But, in fact, I was the one who didn't understand. J.O.N. didn't want sympathy and none of them wanted answers. Nor were they interested in exploring the emotions associated with any of the experiences they had shared. They simply wanted to be heard and accepted. That's the stuff male bonding is made of.

In a matter of days I will deposit my youngest son in a dormitory 875 miles away from home. That's nearly a thousand miles away from his mother, his dog, his weight bench, and his best friends. I've done this before, so I know that the gut wrenching, surgical amputation of the emotional umbilical cord between mothers and sons is inevitable. That's the way it's supposed to be. They're supposed to want to grow up—explore the world independently. And if we've done our jobs right, it will not be as difficult for them to leave us as it is for us to let them go.

So when he says things like "I can't wait to get to school." Or "Mom, you wouldn't believe what the girls in Tennessee look like. It's going to be cool living there," I try to accept that as a sign I have mothered well. But when he says, "I'm going over to Dan's because I won't be seeing him again until Christmas," or "I'm staying over at John's this weekend because it's my last weekend with the guys," I find myself fighting an unfamiliar jealousy.

I grew up with Laurel and Hardy, Bert and Ernie, the Lone Ranger and Tonto, Butch Cassidy and the Sundance Kid. Decades of duos have demonstrated to me the male buddy system, and yet I continued to misinterpret it. I always believed that men communicated on what women consider to be ground level—football fields, Wall Street, alloy wheels. I wasn't convinced that these exchanges were relationship building. I don't think I truly understood the intensity of male friendships until my father lost his best friend.

My father's best friend, Harry, had been a part of my life since long before I was born. For more than fifty years Harry and Dad managed to come together—through a war, marriage, children, and even the loss of a child. I've heard them laugh, shout, and even sing together, but I don't know if they ever talked about their fears, their sadness, or their dreams. I know for a fact they never settled the argument over who scored the most points during St. Theresa's last basketball game. But I do know that since Harry's death, my father hasn't been quite the same. There's a piece of him missing—a place he can no longer go. I know that every time my father hears a funny story he thinks about picking up the phone to share it with Harry. And when he can't, the story loses some of its magic.

In the two years since Harry's death, I've come to understand that he probably knew my father better than any of us do, and that in simply sharing their experience, they shared the secrets of who they really were and hoped to be.

Throughout their childhood, my sons grew up with what they called "The Harry Chronicles"—some of them told by my father, some told by Harry, and others still told by people who knew them both. Through those stories my children and I witnessed the close-up human side of World War II in the South Pacific and Europe. We heard firsthand about the pain of poverty during the Depression and the joy discovered in the simple things we take for granted, like an orange at Christmas. Through their eyes we could see the big bands rising from the floors of movie theaters in New York City. We could feel their competitive spirits when both Harry and my father claimed to be the first to walk across the Hudson River the year it froze solid.

So today, when my son told me he wouldn't be home for dinner because he and J.O.N. were going to camp out and cook hot dogs over a fire, I fought the impulse to count the days we had left together and the need to hang on to him as long as I could. Instead, I told him about the time my father wanted to surprise Harry with a fire in the fireplace while Harry was out sledding with his children on the bank outside their house. While my father had good intentions, he had no experience with fireplaces. It was days before Harry could walk into his house without being assaulted by the smell of smoke. For the next forty years they retold that story every time they sat in front of a fireplace together.

Tonight, when Bryan and his friends sit around a campfire, I have little doubt they will be talking about some things I'd rather not hear and planning adventures I'd rather not witness. But it's really okay with me. Because, someday, around a dinner table or in front of a fireplace, a child or two may learn a lot about life, love, and friendship through the "Bryan Chronicles."

Daddy's Home

Even though I didn't want the divorce, I'm glad it happened. It's a tired metaphor, I know, but when my vision finally cleared, I felt as if I were seeing for the first time in my life. Blinking my eyes at the blinding light like a prisoner emerging from the dungeon after twenty years, I was at first paralyzed with fear and then exhilarated with wonder.

In a way, I wish I had wanted the divorce. At least then I would have been more prepared for it. I would have gathered my strength around me like so many buttresses and my head would have stayed above the torrent of swill that ensued. Instead, I kept getting sucked into it, one raging battle, one brutal soul pummeling after another, until I could scarcely put one foot in front of the other to lead myself out of pain. My two sons were left to find their own way out.

It's ten years now, but in my mind I often see my children as they were then. At nine years old, my youngest son spent much of his time in a world of his own making. Few were invited in, and he came out to me only when he needed affection or affirmation. But every day, between 5:30 and 6 P.M., Bryan would hear his father's voice and bolt in its direction. Even before he was old enough to navigate on his own, the mere sound would set his eyes afire with brightness and ignite his body into movement. For the first nine years of Bryan's life, the words "Daddy's home!" booming through the hallway from the front door carried more magic and more delight than an acre of circus tents. Whatever GI Joe battle raged or Hot Wheels raced, all would freeze or drop to the floor as Bryan hurled himself toward the voice. In the early years his father plucked him from the floor and held him long enough for Bryan to grab his cheeks and plant a kiss on his mouth. Later, as his attention span grew and he could sit in one place long enough to witness a football being carried a full ten yards, he found his place in his father's world. From that day on, Bryan was never without a ball of some kind. He'd prop his head on his football at the base of the couch during football season. February through May, he'd sit and spin the basketball on the tip of his index finger during the NBA games. And in the spring he pounded his catcher's mitt with last year's game ball while he and his father cheered for the Yankees. There seemed a silent language flowing and something bound them as tightly and intimately as if they had exchanged unspeakable secrets.

164

The two of them lived in a world his older brother, Jason, and I could never enter. There were no apparent doors. No discernible pathways, but boundaries nonetheless.

And suddenly, the voice stopped. His father never stepped inside that front door and called to him again. He could have, but he didn't. I believe he thought it would have been too painful for all of us. That a quick and definite break would be easier for them to understand. So, instead, every Tuesday and every other weekend a horn would honk in the driveway, and the boys would stumble out dragging paper bags full of clothes and canvas backpacks full of books.

For years after that, every day between 5:30 and 6 P.M. a funereal pall descended upon our house. We didn't need a clock. Jason and I just knew. Wherever Bryan was in the house, or outside at the basketball hoop, he would stop, deadly still, as if he were listening. Sometimes it would last only a second. Other times, he would seem almost in a trance, as if he were concentrating. He reminded me of my grandmother's mantle clock that had traveled the Atlantic with her in the 1800s and lost its chime along the way. For the next fifty years, the time was accurate to the second, but rather than a musical celebration of the hour, it moaned a laborious hum. The clock maker could never explain why.

As years passed, the horn honked on fewer and fewer Tuesdays. Bryan's half brothers took their place on the floor beside his father's couch in a house Bryan never had a key to. And the word "home" became a place he lived with his mother and brother. We did our best, Jason and I, to fill all the gaps we recognized for each other and for Bryan. I got to know as much about Michael Jordan and Charles Barkley as I knew about my own first cousins, but I couldn't sit long enough through a football game to know a running back from a tight end. I practiced my hook shot and got good enough to give Bryan a run for his money at HORSE, but I never mastered a fastball. I got to most of his ballgames on time and always knew where to find his uniform on game day. But it wasn't my face he wanted to see in the stands. Much of the time I was tired and sad, and often had less patience than desire to give what he needed. Time went on, and as much as we all tried to convince ourselves that we were a family intact, the light in his eyes never quite reached the same brightness.

Tonight, Bryan sits across the table from me in his favorite restaurant. He looks at his watch and we both notice: it's 5:30. I see how much he's changed, but also, judging from his pensive, far-off look, I see how much is unchanged. He is restless and unsettled. He's tried college far from home. He's tried college from home. He's lived with his father, his brother, and now some friends he met in his current job as a waiter. The lonely darkness in his eyes is the same haunted look I saw in a solitary nine-year-old holding a basketball and staring up the driveway at sunset.

The waitress is perky and blonde, her perfectly flawless ivory skin flushes slightly with the telltale glow of flirtation on her cheekbones. She tries to catch his eye. If he notices, he's not letting on. His eyes are lowered and the fingers of his left hand twist the glass in slow quarter turns. "I'm thinking about going out to Colorado," he says. "One of the guys in the apartment is going. Maybe I'll wait tables and take some classes."

"Why out there?" I ask, knowing—in my middle-aged wisdom—that one place is no different from another when your uneasiness is inside you, but not wanting to sound like I've sounded for the twenty years he's been my son. "What would be different from here, or Tennessee where you've already done that?"

He shrugs and glances at his watch and then back down at his glass. "There's nothing keeping me here. Anyplace has to be better than where I've already been." I ache for him, but sympathy has worn thin and a lecture is out of place. I opt for silence. I'm hoping the food comes soon and breaks this spell. Behind him a child's cries rise above the steady din of clinking dishes and muted conversations.

A deep warm voice resonates above the cries. "Come to Daddy," it says. "It's okay. You're okay. See, Daddy's got you now." The cries lower to whimpers and stop. Bryan turns and watches the young father for a second and returns his gaze to the water glass. "So, Mom," he says. "Maybe I shouldn't have quit soccer. What do you think? Maybe my life would have been different."

"I forgot you ever played soccer," I say. "How old were you, ten? Anyway, I thought you hated it."

"Yeah," he says, almost smiling now. "I did." He turns again to check on the baby who is now cheerfully bouncing chunks of meatball on the high chair tray. "You know, when I was little, I sometimes thought Dad left because I quit soccer." He's smiling fully now, but my heart has just fallen to the pit of my stomach. How could I have missed that? Although I recovered slowly from the aftermath of divorce, I thought I had done a fairly good job of back-pedaling. I thought the three of us had said all we needed to say. I wonder what else has gone unspoken and I cringe at the mere suggestion that we may have more hurts to heal, more wounds to apologize for or secrets to bare. For a moment I feel selfish. I am happier with my own life than I have ever been. And it tells me something. The hole my husband left in my life can be filled. The hole in Bryan's can only be patched. Someday, that will have to be enough for him.

"My God," I say, fighting the tears I know are welling. "Why didn't you tell me you felt like that?"

"It's no big deal, Mom. I didn't tell you then because I knew how stupid I sounded." He rolls his eyes and gives me the "give it a rest" look. "Hey, I got over it. Don't worry. I'm not gonna hear voices in my sleep and take a rifle to the roof of the capital building." He adds a chuckle for comic relief. He senses my impending sadness and wants to avert it. He's mastered this art. "Besides, I know why Dad really left."

"Oh, yeah? Why?"

"Because Jason quit baseball."

"Right," I say. "I knew it was something." We both laugh and talk about other things, like how his grandmother used to make rolls like this on Sundays and how nobody makes mashed potatoes as good as mine. I want to bring up Colorado again. I'd like to tell him that changing the scenery won't change his restlessness. That if he keeps mourning a past that should have been, he won't be able to take a single step into his own future. That if he'd just stay put and finish something, he'd know that he's already a very fine young man and he doesn't need anyone else to confirm that for him. But I've said it all before. And I believe, deep down somewhere, he knows it.

167

Outside, we pause before moving toward our separate cars on opposite sides of the parking lot. "Well, maybe if I go to Colorado, I'll take up soccer again," he says as he hugs me and plants a kiss on the top of my head.

"You might," I say, "but as far as I know, there's only one good reason for playing soccer."

"What's that?" he asks, walking backwards.

"Because you like it."

"Hey, I was just kidding, Mom," he says, waving and turning toward his car.

"About Colorado or soccer?" I call back. He's about twenty-five feet away so I can't be sure, but I think he says, "Both."

Sweet Dreams

I'm not sure which came first—that I stopped looking at every man I met from the left hand up or that I realized: I am happy, just plain happy with the way things are.

I go home after work to a house I bought for my youngest son and myself. We picked it out together, inspecting every room and weighing its merit on the character it boasted or lacked. We sent pictures of it to my oldest son at school nine hundred miles away with notes of reassurance that said, "You'll love it, and we promise we won't lose your baseball cards when we pack." Together, my son Bryan and I dismantled a life that was designed for an upwardly mobile family of four and minimized its material volume to better suit an emptying nest. It was a necessary step for both of us and one that, in a sense, set us both free. A house of our own. A mortgage with my name on it, approved on my salary alone. It was exhilarating, and it became the basis of my security.

Bryan, too, could think about his future without worrying how I would manage alone. He would be able talk to me from his dorm room and picture me snug in my tiny den, wrapped in my grandmother's double wedding ring quilt with my Fred Astaire video library stacked beside me. He could relax knowing the next mortgage payment would come easily, even without child support that ended on his eighteenth birthday.

Maybe acknowledging the necessity of my son's independence prompted me to appreciate the value of my own. There were suddenly fewer reasons for wanting a husband. I no longer needed a confidant to support me when I wondered if I had been too hard or too easy on the boys. I didn't need someone to back me up when I had to say "no" to something they wanted desperately to do, but was far too threatening for me to allow. I didn't need someone to take his turn at picking up after basketball practice, or to sit beside me and hold his breath when Bryan shot from the three-point line or Jason hauled his shoulder back and threw the ball home from center field.

Gone at last were the eternal, torturous nights when I could have used someone to lean on as I paced the floor listening for the sound of tires crunching on gravel hours after curfew. No more would I need calm reassurance about the pains of growing up while one of my sons sobbed in his room with his first broken heart. With my youngest child away at college, the house would be empty. The pressure was off.

As much as I longed for companionship for myself throughout the eight years I parented alone, I believe I desired it even more for my sons. There were thousands of curve balls, jump shots, and golf swings that went un-coached and un-praised. In our household there were no coveted Yankee tickets, no man-to-man talks, no advice from the sidelines. I desperately wanted these things for my sons, as much, probably more, than I wanted my hand squeezed under the table at dinner or my cheek brushed with a kiss in the morning.

In those eight years, several men drifted in and out of my life—a few of them more than once. But with each one there was an unsettling, and for a time my life would feel like a jigsaw puzzle that wouldn't lie flat. It puckered up somewhere near the middle as if a piece were jammed in all wrong.

Occasionally, the ending was painful and the ache slow to subside. It surrounded me like a stubborn puddle pooling around my ankles. My kids would tiptoe through it, as if they were afraid to cause a ripple that might catch

170

my attention and make me sad again. But mostly, none of us were much surprised by the sudden silencing of the phone or the resurgence of a neglected hobby of mine like gardening or cross-stitching.

Weeks after I had deposited Bryan more than fourteen hours away from home, I sat and contemplated the enormity of my solitude. I had survived the mourning period of missing him with a hungry emptiness—had memorized his phone number and taught myself not to dial it nightly. Then I sat quietly and waited. The dreaded loneliness never came. Instead, I was met (tentatively at first) by a long neglected unexpected joy. I relished it, because I didn't know how long it would last.

I knew that eventually I would tire of my limitless freedom and find myself haunted by the memory of still-growing feet pounding up the stairway. I might even glance furtively into both my sons' empty rooms and conjure up heaps of sweaty gym clothes in the middle of each floor. But meanwhile I could watch TV or leave it silent, come home from work or go shopping with friends, or work late, or even go out to dinner and not be mindful of saving half to bring home to a hungry child. I could take a nap at 5:30 without anyone worrying that I'm sick and I could have the shower anytime I wanted without planning who would wake up first. And then I noticed. The longing for companionship was as quiet and still as the upstairs hallway.

So, here I am, dreaming dreams of my own. Dreams that don't depend on an empty chair being filled, a nameless face smiling down at me or faceless arms reaching out to me. I stop meeting friends in places where available men congregate. I stop volunteering for boards and committees because it's expected of me. I decide to teach a class at the community college. I take a trip to Vermont alone—a short one, but still it feels like a monumental journey. I tell my friends I will never, as long as I live, attend another singles dance or read another personal ad, and I don't.

I don't look in the self-help section at bookstores anymore. I don't look at the driver to my right at stoplights. I focus straight ahead on where I'm going and I begin to shape my dream. It has a cottage in it, maybe even a cabin, or a bleached cedar cape, filled with art and music. There is water nearby and plenty of time and space for writing or painting, maybe even a little piano by the window. Maybe I'll sit on the bench and play my guitar and teach myself to play "Suzanne" again, like I did when I was in high school.

Out of the Blue

It's pivotal, this moment in my life. At least that's how I describe it to my new-found friend when he sits across the table from me at the Tea Room sipping his ice water with lemon. And I tell him about the sadness long behind me and the wealth of opportunity in front of me while we're sharing a pizza after working late on a project. He understands, he says, because even though he's never been married, he can imagine how much energy it would consume, more than that even, devour, to build a dream and lose it. No, I say, it's not lost. I have two sons and a new life. The dream is not lost; it's just turned into something else. He smiles, a genuine smile, as if he is really happy for me.

The days go by. The projects build. And piece by piece, page by page, my friend and I have come to know each other like a favorite book.

He asks again about my new dream over dessert at the Italian restaurant up the street that he's always wanted to try. Our project is finished and we're celebrating our success. I'm thinking I will miss this new friend now that our work is done. He'll move on to other jobs, other clients. Tomorrow, there will be no reason to see him every other day.

So, he wants to know, how is the plan coming? That new career, the house on the water? It's brewing, I tell him. I'm in no hurry. It's the first time in my life that I don't feel like I'm waiting for something to happen to me—for something to change so I can move on. I'm not waiting for someone to walk into or out of my life, or someone to give me permission.

I'll take it as it comes, I say. I smile, shyly. Suddenly, I wonder why I'm talking about myself so much. It's not my style. I am reserved. Withholding. Now I find I am disclosing with this new friend. Sometimes telling more than I have even told myself. He listens intently. My cynical side tells me he's just being polite.

He twirls his wineglass and we are both silent. I can tell by the way his jaw tightens that he has something on his mind. I've seen this look before.

He needs coaxing, I think, so I break the silence. I tell him I'm going to miss working with him. Miss especially times like this when thoughts and words connect so easily with little regard to which is which. He stops twirling then, and looks at me. His jaw releases into a smile that grabs his whole face and pulls it wide. "That's just what I was thinking," he says. For the first time since I've known him I notice he has very blue eyes.

174

Epilogue

Eight months later . . .

This is how it went:

What do you think about getting married?

What do you mean? What do I think about marriage?

I mean, what do you think about marrying me?

Oh. Well. I don't know. What do you think?

Me?

Yes.

I asked you first.

I know. You always ask me first.

So?

So what?

What do you think about it? I mean, about marrying each other?

I think it would be nice.

Nice? What?

Marrying you. Yeah, it would be nice. I mean, I think I would like that. Was it a proposal or an opinion search?

It was a question.

Not a proposal?

I guess it was.

Was what?

A proposal.

Aren't you supposed to get on one knee?

Me?

Shouldn't one of us? You know, to make it official.

I can't. I'm driving.

Oh. Okay.

Okay what? Was that a yes?

Yes, I guess it was.

We did.

About the Author

Janis Hogan's personal essays have appeared in newspapers in New York and Connecticut and several magazines including *Country Home, Runner,* and *Woman's World.* This is her first published collection. Currently a full-time marketing and public relations consultant, she lives in Connecticut with her husband and is at work on her first novel.